of a
Malcontent

A Collection of Thoughtful, Absurd and Bizarre Correspondence

By J.W. Fagan

Smiling Dolphin Publications

Letters of a Malcontent

A Collection of Thoughtful, Absurd and Bizarre Correspondence

Published by

**Smiling Dolphin
Publications**

**Front and Back Cover Design and Art
by Mark Fitzgerald**

Library of Congress Cataloging-in-Publication Data
Fagan, J.W.
Letters of a Malcontent : A Collection of Thoughtful, Absurd and Bizarre Correspondence / by J.W. Fagan - First Printing
ISBN 1-57502-228-1

**96-68818
CIP**

ACKNOWLEDGMENT

My Grandfather once said to me, "Never believe what you read.". The man himself was one of the most dedicated readers I have ever met - everything from the daily paper to intricate legal documents. He annotated this statement a few seconds later, adding, "Unless YOU wrote it, of course."

That advice was wasted on me at the time, but has rung in my head on a number of occasions since. Especially when it came to the dumpster-loads of junk mail I began receiving when I struck out in the world and my address was sold off to mailing lists all over the country.

You know what I'm talking about, the envelopes of empty promises describing lavish grand prizes, the endless sweepstakes offers, the latest get-rich quick scheme and the products which never quite seem to live up to their advertisements when you DO buy them. All of that contributed to the start of my hobby of harassing the harrasers.

My letters soon strayed from retorting to junk mail and began to include asking questions of all sorts unusual people, places and things. I found also that I was having a ball coming up with these cranks. I still am!

This page is to say thanks to the family, friends, ex-roommates, co-workers, and complete strangers who gave me ideas, encouragement or advice in perfecting the art of poison prank letter. The kudos are too numerous to itemize, so I'll cop out and give an overall "thank you". However, you know who you are and if you know what's good for you, you'll keep it to yourself.

I shall single out Kelly, my wife, for she is the person who made this book happen. Thank you, Kelly! You're the greatest!

The letters are, for a large part, fiction. Remember also that truth is far stranger than fiction, and that I have sprinkled it liberally among the made-up stuff. The names have not been changed to protect the innocent. After all, what fun would that be?

J.W. Fagan
5/1/96

September 9, 1993
810 Myrtle Ave #2
Albany, New York 12208

The Gillette Company
Stationery Products Division
Box 61
Boston, Mass 02199

Attn: Product Manager
     Liquid Paper Division

Dear Madam/Sir,

I have been a customer of your product for going on 8 years now, and have never once had a discouraging word to say about Liquid Paper. I do have a query or two, as well as some suggestions regarding your fluid paper product.

First off, I notice that your corrective fluid bottles come in different colors. In fact, on the side of the Liquid Paper bottle it states "Available in other colors." This sentance is, however, misleading. Liquid paper is white. The Liquid Paper inside the bottle is white no matter what color the outside label is. The black container holds white, the red container holds white, even the green labelled-bottle contains white Liquid Paper! What's up with that? As you can imagine, this variance could lead to an unfortunate mishap, and it has.

In my line of work, I occasionally have need to alter certain colored documents. When I originally purchased a corresponding color-coded label of Liquid Paper I was startled to find the color inside was white! Yikes! However, I found by mixing your product with food coloring, the needed color could be attained. Now when I get a yellowed birth certificate or a pink inventory receipt that needs a touch up, your product serves me well. Even multi-colored immigration paper holds your correective fluid quite well.

My point is that perhaps you should advertise, "Available in other label colors." or "Available in other viscosities." On the other hand, you may wish to experiment with food coloring and try a few different colors yourself. Then you wording will be correct. Another idea I had is that you should put a scent or flavor with the color, like "Bright Banana" or "Precious Plum". The your fluid bottles could read "Available in other great tastes and colors." The possibilities are plentiful.

I look forward to hearing your thoughts on these comments.

Very truly yours,

James W. Fagan

The Gillette Company
P.O. Box 61
Boston, Massachusetts 02199

October 6, 1993

Mr. James Fagan
810 Myrtle Avenue
Apartment 2
Albany, NY 12208

Dear Mr. Fagan:

Thank you for your recent letter concerning the Liquid Paper Correction Fluid. Your comments are being shared with all the people who work on Liquid Paper.

However, Liquid Paper Correction Fluid is currently available in ten colors--Pink, Blue, Green, Ivory, Goldenrod, Ledger Green, Canary Yellow, and other shades of White. These colors may be purchased at your local office supply store. Please refer to the yellow pages of the phone directory under Office Suppliers or Stationers for a retailer that is most convenient to you.

I am enclosing a coupon for Liquid Paper - Stock Color as a small token of our thanks for taking the time to share your feelings with us. Please call me on our toll-free number 1 (800)-Gillette (445-5388) if you ever have any questions or other comments you want to share about Gillette products.

Sincerely,

Diane Catizone

Diane Catizone
Consumer Service Representative

0000130460

Encl:
coupon for Liquid Paper - Stock Color

DICK CHENEY

Dear Friend:

With your help, I want to build an American future which will be brighter than you might think possible right now.

With your help, I ultimately seek to renew the American Dream.

That is why with this letter to you today, I am launching an all-out effort which will include but also go well beyond cutting spending, balancing the budget, rolling back the Clinton taxes, slashing the power, size and expense of government and repairing our defenses.

With your support my goal will be nothing less than to give our children and grandchildren the same secure and opportunity-filled America our parents and grandparents gave to us.

Yes, I realize that on our present course America is heading for serious trouble.

The staggering deficit, the rampant crime, the massive government waste, the decline in our schools, the decaying quality of life, the record tax increases, our floundering foreign policy, our weakened defenses -- I could go on and on. Put simply, I understand why some people believe this is America's eleventh hour.

But coming from Wyoming as I do, and having visited in the last dozen or so months people in over 40 states, I also know the enormous integrity, strength and still untapped potential of the American people.

I know the common-sense and uncommon decency of the vast majority of Americans. And, most important, I know we can reclaim our future if you and I act fast, act forcefully and provide real leadership.

I want and need your help as my partner in this bold fight to put a permanent end to the destructive liberal policies of the last 60 years and launch an American Renewal.

As a former White House Chief of Staff, Congressman from Wyoming, member of the Republican House Leadership and Secretary of Defense, I know what it takes to win important battles in Washington and with your support I am ready to go toe-to-toe with the liberals.

Will you join me? I'll be looking for your Survey and your contribution. Together we can build a future brighter than most Americans dare to imagine right now. Time is short, please answer now.

Sincerely,

Dick Cheney

September 1, 1994
18B Old Hickory Dr. 2B
Albany, NY 12204

Dick Cheney
C/O Alliance for American Leadership
1707 L Street N.W. Suite 333
Washington, D.C. 20036

Dear Dick,

Thanks much for your letter. It really struck a chord.

First of all, you are right. America is in trouble. Government is too big and devoid of common sense. The country is ripe for renewal and reform. Crime is rampant. Liberals are the scourge of this century.

I have done extensive research on the subject of scum Liberals, and found that they can be traced to the witch burnings in Salem. That's right! And also to the fixing of that World Series where the Chicago White Sox threw the game. More recently, Liberal maggots were responsible for the recession in the late 1980's and for Hurricane Hugo. This is not a joke!

I hope you can succeed in your quest to scape up a few bucks from around the country and drive the Liberals back to the Communist pinko states from whence they came!

Although I am unable to contribute to you at this time, please tell me if you have heard of any additional Liberal atrocities. I'm currently compiling a collection for publication and your input would be most welcomed.

Very truly yours,

J.W. Fagan

(NO REPLY RECEIVED)

September 19, 1993
810 Myrtle Ave #2
Albany, NY 12208

President
SANFORD CORPORATION
Bellwood, ILL 60104

Dear Madam/Sir,

I have a query regarding your MAJOR ACCENT highlighter
product, to which I hope you can present a speedy answer.

The other day I was pulling a late night in the office while
pouring over a copy of a deposition I had to summarize for 9:00
a.m. the next morning. I had my Sanford quick reference marker at
ready, highlighting points of interest and importance.
Unfortunately, my exhaustion got the better of me and I was
briefly unconscious for a period of about one hour. When I awoke,
I found that I had the highlighter stuck in my mouth like a
pacifier and, to my alarm, the fluorescent ink had leaked out
onto my tongue and mouth.

Holding your fine product at no fault, I am however
concerned. The day following the incident is blurry and I have
had problems remembering names. At first I thought it was
fatigue, but several bouts of un-induced vomitimg convinced me
that it was something more. Are there properties of this
"flurescent" marker that I should take note of?

I eagerly await your reply.

Sincerely,

James W. Fagan

SANFORD® CORPORATION
Quality Since 1857

2711 Washington Blvd.
Bellwood, IL 60104
708.547.6650   TELEX 6871087
FAX 708.547.5402

September 29, 1993

Mr. James W. Fagan
810 Myrtle Ave. #2
Albany, New York   12208

Dear Mr. Fagan:

I am responding to your September 19, 1993 letter describing your
experience with a Sanford fluorescent highlighter. I can give you
or a treating physician as much information as you need regarding
the chemicals in the inks we use in our Major Accent and Pocket
Accent Markers. However I need to know which marker you were using
and which of the nine colors of ink we make that you were using.
As to whether or not our markers could have caused the symptoms you
experienced, I am not qualified to answer.

Sincerely,

SANFORD CORPORATION

Peter Trucano
Vice President and
     Laboratory Director

PT:pl

PERMANENT MARKERS	SPECIALTY PENS & MARKERS	MECHANICAL PENCILS	WRITING INSTRUMENTS	HIGHLIGHTERS	ADHESIVES THINNERS & SOLVENTS	CONFERENCE ROOM SUPPLIES & ACCESSORIES	CRAFTS & COLORING	STAMP PADS, INKS & PRE-INKED STAMPS	STERLING
	Push & Pull	Logo	Espresso	Major Accent	Rubber Cement	Expo Dry Erase Markers	Mr Sketch	Stamp Pads	Specialt Series
	Penguin	Logo II	Roller Ball	Pocket Accent	Cropot	& Expo Accessories	Fieldsticks	Roll on Ink	Desk Accessories
	Mean Streak	Technician	Calligraphic	Micro Scan	Thinner	Vis A Vis	Ghostwriter	Mini Print	File Boxes
	Bright Sticks	Propel	Pena	Accent Bright		Flip Chart Markers	Erasable	Pom Stamper	Organizers
	Diskribe	Extend	Big Sig	Faccent			Plastic Markers	Numbering Machine	Accu line
	Label Pen	Digd					Nepo	& Checkwriter Ink	School Supplies
	20 20						Oil Pastels		

October 20, 1993
810 Myrtle Avenue
Suite 2
Albany, New York

Dog Warden
City Hall
Albany, NY 12207

Dear Madam/Sir,

   The purpose of this letter is not to complain about the
abundance of stray mongrels in my neighborhood but the lack
thereof. In short, our block needs some strays!

   Our residence is in the Pine Hills section of town and being
here we face a unique ensemble of hazards. Lack of parking, high
taxes and SUNYA students pissing on our plants was one thing, but
our current problem is far more disconcerting. In a word, stray
cats! They are a rampant infestation in the neighborhood, meowing
and whining all the night and roving in packs like unemployed
hoodlums. With no dogs loose in the area, they are free to strut
around and defecate on your porch, usually right on the morning's
Times Union. As you are someone who works with dogs daily, I'm
sure you know that most of the canines you pick up are lost or
abused by uncaring owners, and on the streets through no fault of
their own. Cats, on the other hand, are shiftless gangrels with
no use other than as shammies or floormats.

   What our block needs is some stray dogs to chase the little
furballs up a tree or, better yet, out into traffic where a
delivery truck (which rumble down out streets regularly here) or
a drunk student coming back from the bar at 2am can flatten it.
Years ago, the stray dogs took car of the little muttons, but
with you guys taking them all off the streets, we have to deal
with roving bands of cats who rip into the garbage and hiss at us
taxpayers. They are perpetuated of course by the warmhearted
students who can set out saucers of milk for the damned things.
Often the cats are strays left by their successors from the
previous May who decided the cat wasn't up for the ride to Long
Island and so just let the things out to fend for themselves.

   If there's anything you can do for us, we'd certainly
appreciate it. At the very least, please pass on some poisoning
or trapping information to help us rid our street of these
vermin. I look forward to hearing from you.

                              Yours,

                              J.W. Fagan

June 21, 1994
18B Old Hickory Dr. 2B
Albany, N.Y. 12204

Office of the Mayor
City Hall
Albany, NY 12207

Dear Mr. Mayor,

I wrote to the Dog Warden several months back regarding an issue I felt was very important. Obviously, the Dog Warden did not, for I never received any reply from them.

Granted, they were part of the out-going administration. I would hope that no official under your command takes such an apathetic view toward citizens concerns.

In light of all this, I wish to re-submit my original correspondence to be acknowledged by the current officer in the Dog Warden position. As you may notice, I no longer live in that Pine Hills location. The cats finally drove me out. The situation seems remarkable similar in my current abode, and remains, therefore, a pressing issue. I pray your office gives this the attention it deserves.

Very truly yours,

J.W. Fagan

GERALD D. JENNINGS
MAYOR

CITY OF ALBANY
STATE OF NEW YORK
OFFICE OF THE MAYOR
12207

July 22, 1994

J.W. Fagan
18B Old Hickory Drive, 2B
Albany, NY 12204

Dear Mr./Ms. Fagan,

I have your letter regarding the problems caused in your neighborhood by stray cats. I am forwarding a copy of your letter to the City Clerk's office through which the services of Animal Control are conducted.

I am requesting that the Dog Warden contact you directly to ascertain how we may be of assistance and to take whatever remedial action we can legally accomplish.

I am sure you will be hearing from the Dog Warden soon.

Sincerely,

Gerald D. Jennings

cc: Mrs. Pamela Mineaux

September 23, 1993
810 Myrtle Ave #2
Albany, NY 12208

Product Manager, Refrigeration
SANYO CORPORATION
52 Johnson's Lane
New City, New York 10956

Dear Madam/Sir,

I am familiar with some of your refrigeration products, including your small "apartment sized" units, one of which I own. I have a question regarding your product line, and I hope you can assist me.

My family and I returned from a two week vacation recently to find out that our persian cat, Whiskers, had been inadvertently sealed in the small refrigerator while we were away. By a startling series of events, the person looking after the house had trapped Whiskers in the small fridge unit in the wreck room and "forgot she was in there". To make a long story short, the cat was found by my kids soon after arriving home. It was removed from the unit very docile and quiet, and to be honest, quite frozen.

As Whiskers was a much-loved pet, a back yard burial ceremony was in order. After wrapping our popsicle-like kitty in a blanket I put her in the wood bin in the laundry room until services in the morning. You can imaging the family's shock when Whiskers appeared at breakfast, purring and rubbing against us! I was the most intrigued of the lot, as I had handled Whiskers personally the night before and had no doubts she was stiff-as-a-board dead.

This has sparked my interest in the field of cryogenics and I plan to try several more experiments. I want to use a few other kinds of animals, like a dog or a sheep, to see if this event was more than a just a fluke. However, our present refrigerator just doesn't have the cubic space (and I doubt my wife would go for letting me use the one in the kitchen). I'd be much obliged if you could provide me with brochures regarding units big enough for such animals, and any information you may have regarding this subject. Especially if you've had any other customers currently researching this fascinating topic. I would be interested to hear how their experiments have been coming along.

I eagerly await your reply.

Sincerely,

James W. Fagan

(NO REPLY RECEIVED)

October 14, 1993
810 Myrtle Ave #2
Albany, NY 12208

Manager, Pen Division
BIC Corp.
Milford, CT 06460

Dear Madam/Sir,

Gone are the days of penmanship, and with them, the pens.
Why even this letter, which ten years ago would have most
certainly been in ink or lead, is now done via a laser-spray
contraption of some sort, the workings of which baffle most
Americans.

I for one don't like it. I used to write great letters to my
friends, and often with my Bic pen. I used to have the one where
you could change the color by depressing a notch on the side of
the pen, giving you a choice of four colors instead of just ONE.
It made letters so much more colorful. As well, we used to pull
the ink holders out from the clear plastic pens and use the
shells for spit-ball tubes. The shape was perfect for paper spit-
missiles and the size of the pen great for palming or hiding when
an angry teacher came looking for a culprit.

Another use of those pens was to insert a rubber band inside
the body of the pen casing and expand and contract the rubber
band furiously for one minute, then set the pen down. The pen
would become an instant stink bomb.

Those days are gone, but the memories of creative uses for
writing instruments hasn't died. Just the other day I used one
your round stick mediums to open a bottle of wine. That made me
wonder about the future. I would be interested to know what the
long-range plans for your pen division is, in the face of the
ever-advancing technology. What will Bic be offering to the
writers of tomorrow?

I look forward to your response.

Very truly yours,

J.W. Fagan

October 22, 1993

J.W. Fagan
810 Myrtle Avenue, #2
Albany, NY 12208

Dear J.W. Fagan:

Thank you for your letter. We are very pleased to hear that BIC
pens are giving you high quality performance.

To answer your question about new products, we can assure you that
we are always working hard to meet the ever-changing demands of the
marketplace.   For example, we introduced a special pen with a
cushioned barrel for increased writing comfort.   And, for this
year's back-to-school crowd, we offered new Body Pens, which change
color with the heat from your hand.

We appreciate your taking the time to write to us and we hope you
enjoy the enclosed products with our compliments.

Sincerely,

BIC Corporation

Linda K. Kwong
Public Relations Manager

/lkk

October 20, 1993
810 Myrtle Avenue
Suite 2
Albany, New York
12208

Manager
Harmony Hills Motel
PO Box 241
Scotia, NY 12302

Dear Madam/Sir,

I am writing on behalf of the National Desultory Society to
collect information on your motel in regards to a specific need. Our
group consists of thirty rather well-kept individuals needing lodging
for the period of one week in May, 1994. I am "testing the waters" so
to speak, to get an idea of price range, etc.

Our only specific needs would be a 6 a.m. wake-up call, basic
fitness facilities and perhaps a lap pool. On site meeting and
conference rooms would also be a plus. However, if you have a
licensed bar on the premises, we can overlook the lack of any of the
previous requirements.

The group will be as unobtrusive as possible, though I should
note here that the "Closer" party does tend to get a bit festive. We
will schedule it on Saturday night after the Grievance Report
Banquet, as we have found that it allows everyone to blow off steam
in a healthy way. Despite the low-key demeanor of our group, this
blow-out sometimes surprises proprietors, but let me assure you that
this is a bonded and fully-insured organization.

We would be grateful if you could provide the appropriate forms
and whatnot, I can put something together for our meeting next month.
I'd like to do right by keeping this event local, and support the
local economy. Plus, I have very good connections in the legal field
in these parts.

I look forward to hearing from you,

Very truly yours,

J.W. Fagan

December 1, 1993

JW Fagan
810 Myrtle Avenue
Albany, NY 12208

Dear Mr./Ms. Fagan,

Your letter regarding accommodations puzzled us, as we are a kennel facility and not in the habit of putting up humans. Although our facilities are very nice, you would probably be looking for something with a shower and a bed. There is very little of what you might call "conference space" to speak of, and the noise does tend to be a little excessive here at times. I'm afraid we would definitely not suit your needs.

However, if you find you need a place to keep your pets during your stay here in the Capital District, please consider Harmony Hills.

Yours,

Bert Dunn

October 29, 1993
810 Myrtle Avenue
Suite 2
Albany, NY 12208

Wise Travel Agency
180 Old Louden Road
Latham, New York 12110

Attn: Third World Specialist

Dear Madam/Sir,

I am planning an excursion for early 1994, and would
appreciate it if you could provide some information regarding
destination and travel strategy in locating a underdeveloped
nation to visit.

The end destination is open, really. The parameters of the
choice are fairly few but modest. This may be a relocation (at
least temporarily) and I need access to a few of the modern-world
technologies like world banking and cable television, as well as
running water and electricity. If the area is tropical, I can go
without the running water.

Second, I need a country with a fairly stable government,
that is, no banana republics where leadership changes as often as
the winds. If the leadership is that of a puppet government, like
a CIA-type deal, that would be okay too. At least I'll know those
fellows can be bought.

My mode of transport would likely be spur of the moment,
meaning I need an open-ended departure ticket. Flights only,
please, no boats. I will wish to be at my destination as soon as
possible upon departure, so the few connections and layovers, the
better.

Finally, I need to know what kind of documentation will be
needed. Will I need a passport? And if so does it have to be in
the same name as the ticket-holder? What kind of customs check
will I have to go through? Are their limitations as to how much
cash one can pack in a carry-on bag?

For your services I can pay well, so I would appreciate a
fair amount of discretion and confidentiality in this
transaction. I look forward to hearing your suggestions in this
matter.

Very truly yours,

J.W. Fagan

October 29, 1993
810 Myrtle Avenue
Suite 2
Albany, NY 12208

Wise Travel Agency
180 Old Louden Road
Latham, New York 12110

Attn: Third World Specialist

Dear Madam/Sir,

    I am planning an excursion for early 1994, and would appreciate it if you could provide some information regarding destination and travel strategy in locating a underdeveloped nation to visit.
    The end destination is open, really. The parameters of the choice are fairly few but modest. This may be a relocation (at least temporarily) and I need access to a few of the modern-world technologies like world banking and cable television, as well as running water and electricity. If the area is tropical, I can go without the running water.
    Second, I need a country with a fairly stable government, that is, no banana republics where leadership changes as often as the winds. If the leadership is that of a puppet government, like a CIA-type deal, that would be okay too. At least I'll know those fellows can be bought.
    My mode of transport would likely be spur of the moment, meaning I need an open-ended departure ticket. Flights only, please, no boats. I will wish to be at my destination as soon as possible upon departure, so the few connections and layovers, the better.
    Finally, I need to know what kind of documentation will be needed. Will I need a passport? And if so does it have to be in the same name as the ticket-holder? What kind of customs check will I have to go through? Are their limitations as to how much cash one can pack in a carry-on bag?
    For your services I can pay well, so I would appreciate a fair amount of discretion and confidentiality in this transaction. I look forward to hearing your suggestions in this matter.

                             Very truly yours,

                             O.W. Fagan

Dear Mr. Fagan,

Please refer to Albany Public Library for reference material. Thank you,

MR. GLENN A. WISE
WISE TRAVEL AGENCY
180 OLD LOUDON ROAD
TELEPHONE: 518-783-6011
LATHAM, NY 12110-3996

fingerhut

PRIZE DISTRIBUTION CENTER • 11 McLELAND ROAD • ST. CLOUD, MINNESOTA

Dear Jim Fagan,

We are pleased to inform you that you were confirmed as a winner in our 6-14-93 prize selection -- see below for details on claiming your prize.

In addition, a brand new VCR will be shipped to your 810 Myrtle Ave home if you are one of the fastest in New York to return the enclosed Official Prize Claim/Entry Form.

```
***************** 5-DIGIT 12208
*7181724191 979674* 66 M4711875
.JIM FAGAN
* 2
810 MYRTLE AVE
ALBANY NY 12208
I..II..I.I.I.I.III..I.I..I.I.IIl..I.I.I.I...IIII...I..II
```

You can send for any of these great products when you return your Official Prize Claim/Entry Form. And thanks to your special Pre-Approved Credit status, you don't have to fill out any long, complicated forms — or wait for someone to approve your credit.

If, after trying any selection, you aren't 100% satisfied, just send it back during your FREE Home Trial. You won't owe us a cent. In fact, keep the penny attached to this letter for good luck!

There's no risk or obligation to buy. If you decide to keep your order, you can take advantage of our monthly payment plan and pay in low, easy-to-budget monthly amounts.

Free Gifts with every order is our way of saying thanks to our valued customers. Your first order will bring you 5 FREE GIFTS, yours to keep even if you should decide to return your order.

But whether you order or not, return your Official Prize Claim/Entry Form immediately! You've already won once: your guaranteed prize will be sent upon receipt of your claim. You may win twice: 100 VCR's are waiting for the fastest replies from each state! So hurry, you could be one of our 100 DOUBLE WINNERS!

P.S. Congratulations on your first win! Keep the penny for good luck on the second!

Sincerely,

Ted Deikel

President

September 20, 1993
810 Myrtle Avenue #2
Albany, NY 12208

Mr. Ted Deikel
President
Fingerhut
11 McLeland Road
St.Cloud, Minn 56301

Dear Mr Deikel,

I've waited for some time now to hear from your company
about a prize I supposedly won. What's going on?

Back in June I was sent a letter which said I was a
confirmed winner in the 6-14-93 prize selection. I ripped off a
reply and sent my form back to enable me to win one of the VCR's
you were presenting to the fastest replyer. I even brought my
prize notification notice into work and hung it proudly in my
cubicle. It was the source of much ridicule by my co-workers, but
I had faith in the Fingerhut company name and reputation. You've
never done me wrong, unlike that damn Publishers Clearing House.
You even glued a penny onto the notification page to show I
really was a winner. "I'll show them." I thought.

But now it looks like everyone was right after all. I
entered the sweepstakes with visions of prizes and surprises and
all I got was this lousy penny. "Keep the penny for good luck in
the second draw." the text in your letter said. Yeah, right.

Now, in hindsight, I see stuff in the prize notification
sheet that should have tipped me off. First, it says, "100 VCR's
are waiting for the fastest replies from each state!" HA!
There's only 50 states! What are you going to do with the other
50 VCR's? Who are you trying to kid?

My belief in Fingerhut ain't so good no more. I don't think
I believe that the 30-day trial is obligation free, there's
probably some catch about that, too. What other tricks do you
have up your sleeve? I'm not going to find out and get shafted
again. I learned my lesson. I also should say that I'm not going
to be tooting your praises at my monthly ALONON meetings or to my
Elks Lodge, where I used to leave one of your order booklets in
the john for folks to look through while they did their business.
I just can't honestly do these things when I feel Fingerhut has
given me the bird.

                                    Regretfully yours,

                                    James W. Fagan

fingerhut

11 MCLELAND Rd, ST. CLOUD, MINNESOTA 56395

10/01/93
2231

#A4,243
MR JAMES W FAGAN
#2
810 MYRTLE AVE
ALBANY NY 12208-2659
|..||..|.|..|.|.|||..|..|..|.|.||..|.|.|..|..||||..|..|..||

Dear Mr. Fagan,

Thank you for taking the time to express your views regarding our
Giveaway Programs.

As explained in our Official Giveaway Rules, we design our giveaways
to provide all respondents with an equal opportunity to win. Each
entry must be received by First Class Mail, thus giving all entries a
fair chance at winning.

Unfortunately, giveaways are a game of chance, and although only a
certain percentage of respondents are winners, I encourage you to keep
trying, because all prizes are awarded. The official rules also tell
you how you may obtain a copy of the winners list. Please follow the
directions to ensure that the correct list is sent to you.

I hope this information is helpful and I appreciate the opportunity to
explain our Giveaway Program to you. Thank you for letting us know how
you feel. We do pay attention to what our customers have to say.

                              Sincerely,

                              Customer Service Specialist
                              Fingerhut Corporation

CS/spl

CASH CLAIMS PAYMENT CENTER
ONE ACC CIRCLE • P.O. BOX 6999
REDLANDS, CALIFORNIA 92375-0999

CHARLES C. DELANO
DIRECTOR OF AWARD DISBURSEMENTS

ldlllulhllldulhlllhhlhlllulllhhhullllldl
JW FAGAN
810 MYRTLE AVE APT 2
ALBANY, NY 12208-2659

Dear J. W. Fagan,

      I'm excited to inform you that <u>you have just been guaranteed an award of a brand-new 1994 car or cash in our nationwide "Car or Cash" Sweepstakes.</u>

      IMPORTANT: This letter is your official Award Confirmation. <u>**Please read it carefully**</u>! It contains information that will assist you in claiming your award immediately.

      <u>**You must claim your award by the deadline**</u>! If you fail to do so, we must cancel your award. There are absolutely NO exceptions to this rule!

      According to sweepstakes security procedures, your award designation was computer-logged at the time of name/award selection and coded with an 9-digit "Award Registry I.D. Number." Your personal nine-digit Award Registry Number is listed on the enclosed <u>Award Release Authorization</u> (the green computer "printout").

      When you respond, indicate that Registry Number for identification and retrieval of your award. We can then release your award immediately.

CLAIMING YOUR AWARD: For our "Car or Cash" Sweepstakes with awards ranging from new 1994 cars to rare and valuable U.S. coins to cash awards from $2,500.00 to $1.00 we have simple award claim procedures. Claim by phone or mail, but remember that you must absolutely respond by the sweepstakes deadline!

      On behalf of the Cash Claims Payout Center, all the best to you and your family. Enjoy your award!

                Sincerely,

                Charles C. Delano
                Director of Award Disbursements

December 6, 1993
810 Myrtle Ave #2
Albany, NY 12208

Charles C. Delano
Cash Clains Payment Center
One ACC Circle
PO Box 6999
Redlands, Calif 92375-0999

Dear Mr. Delano,

The arrival of your letter has certainly stirred some excitement around here, let me tell you. Why, the last time I can remember so much hootin and hollerin was when Timmy got hiched up in Worcester.

I've been trying to decide what to do with my cash award, which I guess is jumping the gun a little bit. My friend Leroy says that I won't even get a red cent out of this, but I'm not listening. Leroy never was the sharpest knife in the drawer.

So please don't delay, sent my award as soon as you can. I woulda called but the phone was tuned off by the phone complany last week. Maybe after my cash award we can get that turned back on, eh?

Very truly yours,

J.W. Fagan

NO REPLY RECEIVED

PUBLISHERS
CLEARING
HOUSE

PRIZE PATROL

DAVID SAYER, EXECUTIVE DIRECTOR
PORT WASHINGTON, NY 11050

Dear Friend:

I was glad to see your name on the list of folks who qualify to enter and win
our Ten Million Dollar SuperPrize. Congratulations on your good luck.

As of the moment, thousands of others have already lost out on this opportunity
to be a winner. Unlike you, their names were not picked by our computer to
receive this Bulletin during our selection process. Only people who enter by
the deadline can win the SuperPrize.

> And if yours is the winning entry, it will be the happy privilege
> of our Prize Patrol to present you with the first prize check of
> your Ten Million Dollar SuperPrize in person.

We could even be knocking on your door as early as next month to award the next
$10 Million prize right after the winning number is announced on TV January 28!
So please make sure we have your name and address correct so we can have the check
properly drawn, and hand it over to our winner as quickly as possible.

At Publishers Clearing House, we like to present prize checks in this very
special way. My colleagues and I actually travel to the winner's home wherever
it may be, and arrive at the door with flowers and champagne as well as the
check. You'll recognize us by our blue blazers with the Prize Patrol insignia.

Don't worry about our finding you. We haven't yet missed locating winners and
surprising them with the news of their good fortune. Recently our search took
us to Texas to give Pam Barton her $10,000,000.00 SuperPrize. Pam was away for
the weekend but we surprised her bright and early that Monday morning at her
home -- where you saw her beaming with joy in our commercials!

Which reminds me. One of the things we ask all winners when we arrive is how
they feel about appearing in one of our commercials. You can start thinking
about that possibility right now, and let us know your preference when we arrive
at your door with your first big check if you're our winner.

And don't worry about how you're going to look or act if the Prize Patrol shows
up. Believe me, you'll be surprised -- and delighted! We haven't found a winner
yet who refused the prize money. And I bet you'd be no different.

But first things first. Make sure to return the enclosed entry document by
January 25. If your number is a winner and you do not send it in on time,
the Prize Patrol will be obliged to deliver your SuperPrize to someone else.

But don't even consider letting that happen. Mail your entry today!

Sincerely,

David Sayer

David Sayer
Executive Director
PRIZE PATROL

January 10, 1994
810 Myrtle Ave #2
Albany, NY 12208

David Sayer
Executive Director
PRIZE PATROL
Port Washington, NY 11050

Dear Mr. Sayer,

I was quite excited and chegrined to receive your letter! That is, until I got into the meat of the letter and decided I must decline your generous offer.

All my life I have been "aesthetically challenged", or to call the dog a dog, butt ugly. Your letter raised my hopes of being a winner for the very first time in my feeble life, only to be dashed by the mention of the prize patrol arriving at my hellhole with their bright lights and big cameras. Curses! Foiled again!

Although I know that my reluctant exit from this contest will be marked by no fanfare, I just wanted to let you know why my name won't be pulled from that magic barrel on the drawing day.

Sincerly,

J.W. Fagan

(NO REPLY RECEIVED)

NATIONAL RIFLE ASSOCIATION OF AMERICA

WAYNE LAPIERRE
EXECUTIVE VICE PRESIDENT

Get back to me today and receive a free NRA shooter's cap

Dear Fellow American:

It is my great pleasure to present you with your new NRA membership card. Carry it with pride, you have earned it.

With this card, you'll have access to tremendous money-saving benefits, and a whole range of programs custom-tailored to your interests as a gun owner.

But clearly, the most important feature about this NRA membership card is what it says about YOU.

This NRA membership card says you're an American who believes in good citizenship and safe and responsible firearm ownership.

This NRA membership card says you're one American who will fight to protect your Constitutional right to own a gun.

Most important, this card says you're not going to sit on the sidelines while anti-gun politicians pass one gun control law after another, ban your guns and order their confiscation.

Remember, the NRA is only as strong as your commitment to our gun freedoms. So please, don't put this letter down, hoping to get to it soon. ACT TODAY!

Thanks in advance for your support of the NRA. Please let me hear from you soon.

Sincerely,

Wayne LaPierre
Executive Vice President

P.S. Join the NRA today by returning your membership dues in the enclosed postage-paid envelope today. Or, join immediately by calling 1-800-358-4NRA.

The moment I hear from you, I'll send your NRA Black and Gold shooter's cap--$10.95 value--FREE. Thanks, again, for your support. I look forward to hearing from you.

PPS If you can't afford to join the NRA, then please consider a generous special contribution to help us defend your rights.

April 16, 1994

Mr. Wayne LaPierre
Executive Vice President
National Rifle Association of America
PO Box 96916
Washington, D.C. 20090-6916

Dear Mr. LaPierre,

I was very excited to receive my NRA member card, featuring a smiling eagle on the front, and have shown it to all my friends. They were so impressed, I didn't pay for a drink all night!

You mention "FREEDOM" often and explicitly in your letter, and I couldn't agree with you more. The gun lobby has been hampered by a few rotten apples who have ruined things for the rest of us. But how can the NRA be responsible for "Bob" in Indiana, who's a few french fries short of a happy meal and carries an AK-47 into a supermarket and shoots up the place? I mean, come on.

The Brady Bill is another thing making me sick. A seven day wait for a criminal background check? I don't think so. It's the right of every man, woman and child here in the US of A to own a gun, no matter what they do! Guns don't kill people, people with guns do. I think the anti-gun lobby should bugger off and leave us Americans alone. Actually I think they should be shot, but that would just cause more complications. Thank God you can still go down to the local K-Mart and by a 12-Guage without all that background check crap. They better not try messing that up.

Well, that's what I think. I'm sorry I can't respond positively to your NRA membership today, but as soon as my Mom says (I'm slowly winning her over, maybe next year on my 28th birthday she'll give in) I'm going to get me a full membership and the NRA Visa card, too. Meanwhile my Daisy air rifle will have to do. I would like to get that NRA Shooters Cap you offer for free, I've seen them and they look cool.

Very truly yours,

J.W. Fagan

July 17, 1994
18B Old Hickory Dr. 2B
Albany, N.Y. 12204

Mr. Wayne LaPierre
Executive Vice President
National Rifle Association of America
PO Box 96916
Washington, D.C. 20090-6916

Dear Mr. LaPierre,

Where's my damn NRA shooters cap?

I responded to your offer for a free shooters cap about four months ago, and have not heard from your group since. Your previous letter was bubbling over with enthusiasm about how cool the NRA is, and I agreed. Now I'm getting stiffed.

What's the deal?

Very truly yours,

J.W. Fagan

(NO REPLY RECEIVED)

April 18, 1994

Donald J. Christal, President
270 N. Canon Dr., Ste 1297
Beverly Hills, CA 90210

Dear Mr. Christal;

I wish to express a few sentiments about your product, California Tan.

First of all, it didn't work for me. I applied generous, even coats of the "Triple Action, Multiple Strength" lotion and I'm still white as rice. No matter how often I used it, or how I let the formula seep in, no brown, tan or off-white coloring resulted.

Due to my experiences with tanning, I was skeptical from the onset of my little experiment with your product. Due to my fair skin, I had been warned by my physician not to try tanning under the harmful rays of the sun which turned my pale glow to red meat in minutes. I then tried those other "rub on tan" products and had been laughed at by co-workers and family members alike. Undaunted, I tried tanning beds, but I was again burned. My only hope for a healthy glow was a lotion that required no exposure to the sun, and I thought with your "California Tan" product that I had found it. I guess when something is too good to be true, it is.

Looking ahead, I guess I'll have to learn to deal with my "office tan" and look forward to the next winter season.

Very truly yours,

J.W. Fagan

CALIFORNIA TAN

6 May 1994

Mr. James Fagan
810 Myrtle Avenue, #2
Albany, NY 12208

Dear James,

Thank you for your letter dated April 18, 1994.

The product you used, Fever, is 100% guaranteed. Fever is scientifically proven to give you up to 10 times better tanning results in half the time. This product is also designed for usage in the tanning beds only.

I am sending you a packet of our Self-Action Self-Tanning Gel which will give you a golden brown tan without the sun. For best results, apply a thin coat of Self-Action in even circular motions to your face, neck and body.

We are sorry for any inconvenience this may have caused you.

Sincerely,

Carol Wise

Carol Wise
Marketing Assistant

Heliotherapy The Positive Effects of The Sun™

California Tan's Scientific Research Center 1100 Glendon Ave., Suite 1250 Los Angeles, CA 90024 310-824-2508 • 800-SUN-CARE • FAX 310-824-0082

April 17, 1994

Manager, Product Development
Colgate-Palmolive Consumer Affairs
300 Park Avenue
New York, NY 10022

Dear Madam/Sir;

I wish to share with you an experience which not only enriched my dental brushing routine, but could lead to an exciting new product line for your fine company.

Less than a week ago, I shuffled into the washroom to slash some water on my face and preform the other morning duties. I squirted a gob of paste on my toothbrush and proceeded to vigorously scrub my pearly whites as I do. After a rinse and spit, I noticed a tingling sensation I wasn't accustomed to. It was like a spearminty-hot sort of feeling, and it also seemed to effect the inside of my cheeks similarly.

Well, imagine my suprise when I checked my toothpaste tube to find that it was in fact NOT my toothpaste but muscle rub! I had mistaken the similar tubes in my morning groggy state. At first I was concerned with the effects this might have on my gums and skin, but aside from having a slightly slurred speech, no ill effects presented themselves.

This has led me to experiment. By mixing a little COLGATE and muscle rub on my toothbrush, not only have my teeth been whiter than ever, but my mouth feels refreshingly minty cool. I suggest you investigate this, and perhaps integrate some of the muscle rub's ingredients into your fine product. I'm sure your other consumers would be interested in the change, although you could make a separate product to avoid losing those die-hard fans of the original Colgate. Maybe something along the lines of "New Colgate" and "Classic Colgate".

If I can be of assistance in your research or marketing study work, please do not hesitate to contact me.

Very truly yours,

J.W. Fagan

COLGATE-PALMOLIVE *COMPANY*
A Delaware Corporation

300 Park Avenue
New York, NY 10022-7499
Household Products
800-338-8388
Personal Care Products
800-221-4607

Consumer Affairs Department

April 25, 1994

Mr J.W. Fagan
#2
810 Myrtle Avenue
Albany, NY 12208

Dear Mr Fagan:

Thank you for contacting us. The comments and suggestions that
consumers make about our products and our company are important to us
and are sent to the appropriate department for consideration.

We appreciate your taking the time to contact us. Please accept the
enclosed with our compliments.

Sincerely,

Chris Gitelson
Consumer Representative
Consumer Affairs

CKG/nal

Enclosure
0272254A

September 4, 1994
18B Old Hickory Dr. 2B
Albany, N.Y. 12204

Chris Gitelson
Consumer Affairs Department
Colgate-Palmolive Company
300 Park Avenue
New York, N.Y. 10022-7499

Dear Chris,

Well, it's been several months since I shared my idea for an "improved" Colgate, and I haven't seen it on the shelves out this way. What's the hold up?

Just to bring you up to speed, I have been using my mixture of muscle rub and Colgate as a tooth paste for over eight months now, and have suffered no ill effects. Every morning, my mouth is alive with a tingly freshness so enthralling it's hard to find the right word to describe it. Gratifying? Delightful? Tangy? I'm not sure. The only small side effect I can detect is that my speech is slightly drawled for an hour or so after brushing, due to some elements of the muscle rub I haven't yet pinned down. But, I'm still working on it.

Your letter seemed to infer that your company was rather excited by my idea, and that led me to believe that I might be able to get my special "potion" off the shelves of my local druggist, as made by Colgate. That's what has prompted me to write in and check on things. Are you folks still moving ahead with the product?

On a personal note, I hope your summer was enjoyable and you stayed out of the sun. Tan's may look healthy but it's skin cancer, and there ain't nothing healthy about that.

Very truly yours,

J.W. Fagan

May 29, 1994
18B Old Hickory Dr. 2B
Albany, N.Y. 12204

Customer Comments
KELTY, Incorporated
New Haven, MO 63085

Dear Customer Comments,

I recently purchased a Kelty Arapaho backpack. My decision to buy this particular backpack was mainly because I was impressed by the durable qualities of the pack. Also, my girl liked the color.

While hiking not a week later in the wilds of New York City, I was accosted by a hungry pack of juvenile delinquents. Remembering all of the warnings about giving them handouts, I tried to exit the situation without provoking them. Apparently, I had come between them and their cubs, or something like that, for they were relentless in their pursuit through Grand Central Station. I tried to use the "climb a tree" adage, but found to my chagrin that there are very few trees down there in the subway.

As they circled me, I took the pack off and held it in front of me, hoping to fend them off or at least soften the expected blows/gunfire. The pack did indeed draw their attention, and they proceeded to relieve me of its ownership. With a few parting snarls, they retreated to the green line subway, leaving me pack-less, though with my health intact.

I thought you might like to know that your pack aided in my survival, and I am sure that if it can perform that well in a jungle, that the great outdoors would be child's play. I'm already saving up for another Kelty pack, so please send me a brochure on the new styles when they come out.

Very truly yours,

J.W. Fagan

KELTY. DEALER LIST

For 1994, our catalog format has been designed to provide vital information while minimizing waste, in addition to providing superior product lines and thoughtful customer service. The intelligent use of our Natural Resources is a critical aspect of the *Kelty Philosophy*. The enclosed catalog outlines general specifications for our **entire line** of Expedition, Backcountry and Open Trail Kelty Hard Gear Products.

We urge you to visit your local Kelty Dealer to see the products. All of the Kelty dealers will have either the product in the store or at the very least, a color catalog containing **all** of our products. <u>Note</u>: All of our dealers can special order any product at any time ... just ask! Or if you choose, please call us at **1.800.423.2320** to receive specific information for any of our products. A specification sheet will be sent to you via FAX or Mail. This will include a picture as well as all of the information needed for you to *shop at home* before you purchase your Kelty product.

Alaska		California (cont.)		(cont.)	
ANCHORAGE	BARNEY'S SPORT CHALET	BERKELEY	SIERRA DESIGNS		
	GARY KING, INC.	BISHOP	WILSONS EAS...		/Y STORE
	RECREATIONAL EQUIPMENT, INC.	BREA	...		1ENT, INC
EAGLE RIVER	BOONDOCK SPORTS	BURI...			
FAIRBANKS	ALASKA SPORTSMAN'S MALL, IN				
	BEAVER SPORTS INC				
JUNEAU	FOGGY MTN SHOP				'NG
KODIAK	MACK'S SPORT SHOP				
PALMER	PALMER SPORTS				
	PEMPEK'S GUN SALES				
SOLDOTNA	WILDERNESS WAY				
SITKA	WINROSE ENTERPRISES				
VALDEZ	BEAVER SPORTS				
WASILLA	CHIMO GUNS ETC				
Alabama					... INC
AUBURN	SOUTHERN TRAILS				... MOUNTAINEERING
BIRMINGHAM	ALABAMA OUTDOORS				SPORTMART
	BIRMINGHAM SPORTS UNLIMITED			...N CARLOS	RECREATIONAL EQUIPMENT, INC.
	OVER THE MTN OUTFITTERS			SAN DIEGO	ADVENTURE 16
	ROGER'S TRADING POST				RECREATIONAL EQUIPMENT INC
FLORENCE	SOUTHEASTERN DIVERS INC.				SPORT CHALET
HUNTSVILLE	WILEY OUTDOOR SPORTS				SPORTMART
MOBILE	MOBILE SPORTS UNLIMITED		..URTMART	SAN DIMAS	RECREATIONAL EQUIPMENT INC.
	SPOKE 'N TRAIL, INC.	...ALLEY	MARK SPORTS	SAN FRANCISCO	COPELAND SPORTS
MONTGOMERY	SOUTHERN TRAILS		SPORTS FEVER		G & M SALES, INC.
TUSCALOOSA	CYCLE-PATH,INC.	HAWTHORNE	SPORTMART		LOMBARD'S SPORTS
Arkansas		HEMET	B J SPORTING GOODS	SAN JOSE	CEDAR PEAK OUTFITTERS\TRADING
FAYETTEVILLE	PACK RAT OUTDOOR CENTER	HUNTINGTON BEACH	SPORT CHALET		MEL COTTON'S SPORTING GOODS
LITTLE ROCK	LITTLE ROCK SPORTS UNLIMITED		SPORTMART		REED'S SPORT SHOP
	LOCKWOOD'S SPORTMART	KENTFIELD	MARMOT MOUNTAIN WORKS		SPORTMART
Arizona		LA CANADA	SPORT CHALET INC		WESTERN MOUNTAINEERING
FLAGSTAFF	PEACE SURPLUS INC	LA MESA	BLACK MOUNTAIN OUTFITTERS	SAN LEANDRO	COPELAND SPORTS
GRAND CANYON	BABBITT BROS. TRADING COMPANY		SPORT CHALET		SPORT CHALET
PHOENIX	ARIZONA HIKING SHACK	LIVERMORE	SUNRISE MOUNTAINEERING INC	SAN LUIS OBISPO	COPELAND SPORTS
	POPULAR	LOS ANGELES	ADVENTURE 16		MOUNTAIN AIR SPORTS,THE
PRESCOTT	BASECAMP DIVISION		SPORT CHALET	SAN RAFAEL	COPELAND SPORTS
SEDONA	CANYON OUTFITTERS	LOS ANGELES	SPORTMART		MARIO OUTDOOR
	GO TAKE A HIKE SPORTS	MAMMOTH LAKES	DOUG KITTRIDGE SPORTING GOODS	SANTA ANNA	SPORTMART
TEMPE	RECREATIONAL EQUIPMENT INC		FOOTLOOSE, INC.		RECREATIONAL EQUIPMENT INC
TUCSON	BOB'S BARGAIN BARN, INC.		VILLAGE SPORTS CENTER	SANTA BARBARA	COPELAND SPORTS
	THE SUMMIT HUT	MARINA DEL RAY	SPORT CHALET		GREAT PACIFIC IRON WORKS
California		MENDOCINO	ADVENTURE STORE, THE		THE MOUNTAIN AIR SPORTS
ANTIOCH	GREAT OUTDOORS, THE		THE OUTDOOR STORE	SANTA CLARITA	SPORT CHALET
ARCATA	ADVENTURES EDGE	MERCED	T.O.E.	SANTA CRUZ	BUGABOO MOUNTAIN SPORTS
	PRO SPORT CENTER	MISSION VIEJO	SPORT CHALET		
AUBURN	SIERRA MTN. SPORTS	MODESTO	VALLEY SPORTS		
BAKERSFIELD	BIGFOOT MOUNTAINEERING				
	COPELAND SPORTS				
BASS LAKE	SUMMIT ADVENTURE				
BERKELEY	COPELAND SPORTS				
	MARMOT OF CALIFORNIA				
	RECREATIONAL EQUIPMENT INC				

[Handwritten note:]

Jin,
Sorry about your loss - at least you have your health! Here is the latest product list you requested.
Sharon

PACKS. SLEEPING BAGS. TENTS. OUTDOOR INGENUITY.

American Inventors Corporation
82 Broad Street
Westfield, MA 01086-1616
(413)568-3753

- Invention Counseling

- Patent Services

- Design Assistance

- Marketing Services

- Technology Transfer

May 19, 1994

J W Fagan
810 Myrtle Avenue
Suite 2
Albany NY 12208

RE: F068999

Dear Mr. Fagan:

We recently responded to your request for information about our professional services by mailing you
an informational brochure. We have not received
your reply as yet.

There is a good possibility that your idea may have
commercial potential, and a response now could lead
to establishing your prior right to the idea. This
can only happen if you complete and return the
Record and Disclosure form.

Since 1975, we have provided experienced, professional guides and counselors for idea people. The first
step in this process is for you to get our FREE professional assessment of your idea. Confidentiality
is guaranteed, and there would be absolutely no
obligation to you.

If you have any questions, need assistance in completing the Record and Disclosure form, or just did
not receive your packet, please call our Marketing
Department toll-free at 1-800-338-5656, extension
950. We can be reached between 9AM and 5PM, Eastern
time.

We look forward to hearing from you soon.

Sincerely,

Michael Lane
Marketing Director

ML/rw

May 25, 1994
18B Old Hickory Dr. 2B
Albany, N.Y. 12204

Michael Lane
Marketing Director
American Investors Corp.
82 Broad Street
Westfield, MA 01086-1616

Dear Mike,

Thank you for your letter last week, it was good to hear from you. As your suggested, my idea may have commercial possibilities, and I am very cautious about to whom I share this idea with. Your assurance of confidentiality has won me over, so here's my idea.

How many times have you gone to work and looked in the mirror to see you missed a few hairs while shaving. Or maybe cut yourself with the razor while running late? Well, those days are over. I have developed a hair removing gel (not a NAIR product, but entirely different ingredients) that can be applied to the face and/or other furry areas and remove unwanted growth in 30 seconds. Here's how it works.

After applying SHAVEGEL (as I like to call it), the user puts on a plastic mask to cover the gel. This activates the gel. Thirty seconds later, the user removes the mask, washes their face and they are done. This process will also translate to other body hair removal, with the appropriate body mask to activate the gel.

The mask/body mold would be re-usable, and inexpensive. The active ingredients of this product do not irritate skin or produce heat. I've tested it on eight different subjects and had not complaints or incidents. I'm sure there will be no problem with the FDA on this.

No more leg waxing, tweezers or sharp blades! This product will be sought by anyone who's ever sliced themselves open with a blade, or had hair ripped out by the roots. Can you imagine the market in the summer months alone?

I'd be interested in hearing your opinion of this product, and will continue testing in the meantime. I look forward to hearing from you.

Very truly yours,

J.W. Fagan

American Inventors Corporation
82 Broad Street
Westfield, MA 01086-1616
(413)568-3753

- Invention Counseling

- Patent Services

- Design Assistance

- Marketing Services

- Technology Transfer

June 3, 1994

J W Fagan
18B Old Hickory Drive
#2B
Albany, NY 12204

RE: F068999
     "SHAVEGEL"

Dear Mr. Fagan:

Thank you for sending us your invention, which has
been reviewed by our engineering department.
We feel the idea may have some potential, however,
we need some additional information in order to
assess it properly.

The requested information is marked below with an
"X":

More detailed or clearer drawing,
showing internal parts, if applicable.

More detailed electrical information.
Include a circuit drawing and parts list.

Sketch of game board with coloring
scheme.

Set of rules explaining how the game is
played.

Method of installation or application.

X   Complete formula with ingredients.

Description of how to use your invention.

Working computer program or program disk.

Please mail the information to us as soon as possible
so that we may expedite the assessment.
You may use the back of this sheet or additional
paper.

Sincerely,

Jeff Rehbein /cb
Jeff Rehbein
Marketing Department

cb

June 6, 1994
18B Old Hickory Dr. 2B
Albany, N.Y. 12204

Jeff Rehbein
Marketing Department
American Inventors Corp.
82 Broad Street
Westfield, MA 01086-1616

Dear Jeff,

Thank you for your letter last week. Although it was good to hear from you, I wondered why Mike Lane wasn't able to write back. Hope he hasn't fallen ill, or worse, been laid off.

The gist of your note was that you need more information, specifically my secret ingredients, in order to "assess" the potential of the product. Since my last correspondence, I have tested SHAVEGEL on three more people (among them, a severely hairy individual who wished to loose it all) and all successfully shed the body hair. Painlessly, I might add, and in 30-40 seconds. Since switching to human subjects for the testing, the results have been even more positive, and my dog has enjoyed being allowed to grow his hair back in.

I understand your request for information, but you need to see it from my side. If I give you the ingredients, why would you need me? I would see my SHAVEGEL on the market under another name and still be living on social security while some fat cat in Westfield, Mass rides the SHAVEGEL wave of success. No sir. No can do. At the very least, I can open a non-electric electrolyses chain myself and go that route.

But, I confess I'd much rather prefer to work with a reputable, professional company such as yourselves. Can't we work this out?

Very truly yours,

J.W. Fagan

American Inventors Corporation
82 Broad Street
Westfield, MA 01086-1616
(413)568-3753

• Invention Counseling

• Patent Services

• Design Assistance

• Marketing Services

• Technology Transfer

June 13, 1994

J W Fagan
18B Old Hickory Dr
#2B
Albany NY 12204

RE: F68999

Dear Mr. Fagan:

We have been unable to reach you by phone. Please call
us toll free at 1/800-338-5656 at your earliest
convenience.

Sincerely,

Jeff Rehbein
Marketing Department

JR/djj

June 15, 1994
18B Old Hickory Dr. 2B
Albany, N.Y. 12204

Jeff Rehbein
Marketing Department
American Inventors Corp.
82 Broad Street
Westfield, MA 01086-1616

Dear Jeff,

I'm sorry to hear that you have been having trouble reaching me by phone. Perhaps that is due to the fact that I don't have one.

I conduct all my business through written correspondance, as to prevent misunderstandings, misconceptions and to get everything in writing. It's like my great Grandaddy used to say. "If you can't spit on your hand and shake on it, it ain't a deal."

So let's do this. I'll spit if you will.

Very truly yours,

J.W. Fagan

American Inventors Corporation
82 Broad Street
Westfield, MA 01086-1616
(413)568-3753

- Invention Counseling

- Patent Services

- Design Assistance

- Marketing Services

- Technology Transfer

August 31, 1994

J W Fagan
18B Old Hickory Drive
#2B
Albany, NY 12204

RE: F068999
     "SHAVEGEL"

Dear Mr. Fagan:

Recently we sent you a letter requesting additional information on your invention. The information you sent us in the disclosure document does not contain enough detail or description for a proper evaluation.

Please forward the information indicated below if you wish us to continue with the free evaluation of your invention. We cannot continue until we receive this from you.

The requested information is marked below with an "X":

    More detailed or clearer drawing, showing internal parts, if applicable.

    More detailed electrical information. Include a circuit drawing and parts list.

    Sketch of game board with coloring scheme.

    Set of rules explaining how the game is played.

    Method of installation or application.

X   Complete formula with ingredients.

    Description of how to use your invention.

    Working computer program or program disk.

Please mail the information to us as soon as possible so that we may expedite the assessment. You may use the back of this sheet or additional paper.

Sincerely,

Jeff Rehbein
Marketing Department

September 4, 1994
18B Old Hickory Dr. 2B
Albany, N.Y. 12204

Jeff Rehbein
Marketing Department
American Inventors Corp.
82 Broad Street
Westfield, MA 01086-1616

RE: F068999
    "SHAVEGEL"

Dear Jeff,

Your latest letter, asking again for my formula to my SHAVEGEL, has me baffled. I thought we covered this already.

As I explained, the ingredients of SHAVEGEL are highly secret, hence the reason why I want to patent it. If I "spill the beans" to you, it won't be secret, will it?

Now look, Jeff. I'm not saying your company can't be trusted. It's just that I've heard stories. Like the one about the guy who invented Post-It Notes only to have it swiped by 3M, the company he approached to make the glue substance for him. He could've been up to his ears in babes, bubbles and greenbacks by now, but instead he can't go to a family reunion without someone placing a yellow sticky-note on his back with "Kick me, Please!" written on it.

Confer with Mike Lane and let's get on with this. Enough stalling already. Both Chesebrough-Ponds and Gillette Company want me to sell the recipe to them, and I'd like to have this baby protected before I go handing the secret over.

                              Very truly yours,

                              J.W. Fagan

American Inventors Corporation
82 Broad Street
Westfield, MA 01086-1616
(413)568-3753

- Invention Counseling

- Patent Services

- Design Assistance

- Marketing Services

- Technology Transfer

September 15, 1994

J W Fagan
18B Old Hickory Drive
#2B
Albany, NY   12204

RE: F068999
      "SHAVEGEL"

Dear Mr. Fagan:

Your invention has been reviewed by our Engineering Department. Taken as a whole we feel
it does not meet our criteria for representa-
tion.

We have stringent rules for accepting new
ideas. Even though an idea may have merit it
may not meet all of our criteria.

Most inventive people come up with ideas from
time to time. If at some point in the future
you wish to submit another idea to us for assessment, please do so. Simply submit your
idea on paper using your complete name and
address. We will maintain all additional ideas
in your original file.

We thank you for considering American Inventors
Corporation and we look forward to hearing from
you in the future.

Sincerely,

Jeff Rehbein /cb
Jeff Rehbein
Marketing Department

cb

May 1, 1994
18 B Old Hickory Drive-2B
Albany, NY 12204

Manager, Product Services
DANA LIGHTING
50 United Drive
West Bridgewater, Mass 02379

Dear Madam/Sir,

I recently purchased a halogen torchiere from a popular department store chain (Caldor) and I wish to express my pleasure with your product and share an idea I had concerning it.

At first, we used it as an ordinary living room light, until my friend pointed out that the light looked so bright you could probably get a tan from it. Sure enough, with a few modifications, we've rigged the lamp to provide great tanning capabilities. After only three half-hour sessions, both myself and my friend have noticed improved skin coloration and healthy shine. I wouldn't have believed it, but now I do.

I think you folks should consider marketing this lamp with a swing-arm so the light can be pivoted over a bed of some sort, as standing is far less comfortable. Perhaps you have already designed such a device and you have it for sale? I would be interested to know. If not, please contact me and I will gladly shared my discoveries with you.

I look forward to your reply.

Sincerely,

J.W. Fagan

50 United Drive
West Bridgewater, MA 02379
Telephone (508) 584-1122
FAX   (508) 584-4927

A DIVISION OF CATALINA LIGHTING, INC.

Date: 6/14/94

  To: J.W. Fagan

From: Customer Service Dept.

  Re: Floor Lamp

===

Dear J.W. Fagan:

We are in response to your recent letter.

Please be advised that we do not recommend that you utilize
this product for tanning. This was not the intended use
when this lamp was manufactured, and any diversion from the
specific use (to illuminate a room), will be done at your
own risk. This product is not sold with any such claim - as
to be used as a tanning product.

Best regards,

DANA LIGHTING, INC.
CUSTOMER SERVICE DEPT.

June 26, 1994
18B Old Hickory Dr. 2B
Albany, N.Y. 12204

Joseph Victori Wines, Inc.
MISTIC WINES Division
Customer Service
1 Farcette Drive
Del Rio, TX 78840

Dear Madam/Sir,

I'm writing to congratulate you on your new product, "MISTIC".
Though I myself have not tried your beverage, there is the chance
I may. However, I didn't write concerning that. It is about your
advertisement of "MISTIC" that I send this letter.

The ad reads "Go Naked" and features two figures; a guy on a
surf board with "Surf Naked" across his midsection, and a woman
roller blading with "Skate Naked" across her. Now I will conceded
that "Go Naked" is a clever and catchy slogan, but think about it.
Skate naked? Obviously you've never been on roller blades.

I can't talk to the surf naked thing, because I think surfing
is already done mostly naked anyways. But if you've ever had a
spill on blades, you'd know skating naked would be like playing
catch with a roll of barbed wire while bare-handed. Naked roller-
blading would take just one fall to give you road-rash so bad you'd
never have kids.

Although I may try your drink in the future, there is no way
in hell I'm going to "skate naked". I'm not going to even joke
about it.

Very truly yours,

J.W. Fagan

ROYAL

Mistic

Premium Natural Beverages

July 26, 1994

J.W. Fagan
18B Old Hickory Drive, 2B
Albany, NY 12204

Dear J.W. Fagan:

Thank you for your letter of June 26 regarding our Mistic "Go Naked" print advertising.

Needless to say, we are not suggesting that people literally "go naked." Neither do we expect that they will "surf naked" or "skate naked" as a result of seeing our ad. We simply mean to suggest that, whatever they are doing, a cool refreshing, all-natural Mistic will enhance the experience.

We are enclosing herewith a Mistic "Go Naked" T-shirt as a token of our thanks for your interest in our product and advertising.

Cordially,

Bill Roethel
Vice President, Marketing

Enclosure

g:wpsales/brjwf.ecm

Joseph Victori Wines, Inc.

2525 Palmer Avenue, New Rochelle, N.Y. 10801 • 914-637-0400 • FAX: 914-637-0420

June 19, 1994
18B Old Hickory Dr. 2B
Albany, N.Y. 12204

Thomas H. Ebele, D.M.D.
344 Delaware Avenue
Delmar, NY 12054

Dear Dr. Abele,

The old chompers aren't what they used to be, and I'm hoping you can help.

I usually try and make it in to a dentist's office for a cleaning every few years, but of late I have been remiss. I floss and brush regularly, and retain a hollywood smile despite the relentless marching of time. My question, however, relates more to the efficiency of my teeth, as opposed to the aesthetics. In other words, I can't grind the meat like I used to anymore. I've opened one too many bottle caps with the old ivories and they don't seem to tear into Big Mac's the way they used to.

My question is this; can I come in for a sharpening of my teeth, and how much will it set me back? Or, alternatively, is there an "in home" process for filing the incisors to give them their (pardon the pun) bite back? If so, do you provide such a kit? I look forward to hearing from you.

Very truly yours,

J.W. Fagan

Delmar Dental Medicine

DR. THOMAS H. ABELE, D.M.D.
DR. GEOFFREY B. EDMUNDS, D.D.S.
344 DELAWARE AVENUE
DELMAR, NEW YORK 12054
439-4228

June 29, 1994

J.W. Fagan
188 Old Hickory Drive-2B
Albany, NY 12204

Dear Mr. Fagan:

I'm writing in response to your letter dated June 19,1994. You were requesting information on any process we may have available to "sharpen" your teeth, either in the office or at home. It is a fact that as people grow older, their teeth will begin to loose their "edge". Unfortunately, there are no means available in dentistry today to do such a treatment.

We do recommend patients have a regular dental exam and cleaning twice a year, depending on their dental health, however, we are aware of some patient's inability to attend regularly. We are very pleased that you took the time to write and pose such an interesting question.

Should you wish to have any input on your dental health and any recommended forms of treatment, please feel free to contact the office at any time. We will be glad to assist you in any way that we can.

Sincerely,

Thomas H. Abele, D.M.D.

June 8, 1994
18B Old Hickory Dr. 2B
Albany, NY 12204

Chef Boyardee
C/O American Home Food Products, Inc.
685 Third Avenue
New York, N.Y. 10017

Dear Chef,

I watch lots of t.v. and have followed your life story in the Chef Boyardee commercials. You're a hero of mine!

When you were in the Italian orphanage you stood by your beliefs about making good food that kids like. My Mom used to buy Spaghettio's every week, and occasionally the Ravioli, too. But recently, she has stopped using our food stamps for your pasta products, claiming that it is too expensive. My little sister MaryEllen had lots of medical work done recently, something called "rinkles" or "rickets" she got at school. So now we eat a lot of roughage and berries that we grow or find. My brother Timmy hates vegetables and dairy products and has gotten very skinny lately. I miss your food a lot, too.

What I want to ask you is could you send me the recipe for your Spaghettio's so I can make it for my family. We grow tomatoes and my friends Mom gives us pasta she makes. So we just need to know what you put in besides that. When I grow up, I plan to join the army and try to get stationed in Italy, then learn how to cook real good like you. I know you don't really cook all the Spaghettio's yourself, but you came up with it.

If this letter isn't great I'm only learning how to do this at school. Please write me back.

Your friend,

J.W. Fagan

AMERICAN HOME FOOD PRODUCTS, INC.

FIVE GIRALDA FARMS

MADISON, NJ 07940-0873

July 11, 1994

Mr. J. W. Fagan
18 B Old Hickory Drive 2 B
Albany, NY 12204

Dear Mr. Fagan:

Thank you for contacting American Home Food Products.

As you would expect, we place a great value on the opinions of
our consumers. So, we were truly delighted to hear how much
you enjoy Chef Boyardee.

We hope you will continue to enjoy our many fine products.
Please accept the enclosed with our thanks.

Sincerely,

Marie Briggi
Consumer Affairs Representative

Ask someone what his favorite type of food is and very often the answer is Italian. This popular cuisine is one of America's most loved, equally enjoyed by young and old. Supermarket shelves feature hundreds of pastas, spaghetti sauces, canned and frozen entrees, pizzas, etc. This vast selection was not always available. In fact, until the 1930s, most Americans could find Italian food only in restaurants.

One person who deserves credit for popularizing and introducing generations of Americans to Italian - style food is Hector Boiardi, the founder of Chef Boyardee. During the 1930s and 40s he originated the first nationally available spaghetti dinner and Italian sauce products. In 1938, he closed his successful Cleveland restaurant to devote full effort to marketing his line of packed Italian foods.

An Italian immigrant, Hector Boiardi came to the U.S. at the age of 17, already having 6 years of experience in the hotels and restaurants of his native northern Italy. Mr. Boiardi came to this country at the urging of his older brother Paul who had arrived a few years earlier. The great Italian singer, Enrico Caruso, was a friend of the Boiardis and encouraged them to come to America.

Before turning 35, Hector had been head Chef at the finest restaurants in New York, catered President Woodrow Wilson's wedding reception at the Greenbriar Hotel in West Virginia, opened a successful restaurant in Cleveland and began selling Italian foods for home use.

At the Cleveland restaurant, customers entered and left through the kitchen. As they were leaving, Hector would ask how they enjoyed the meal, especially the spaghetti. It wasn't long before customers were asking for portions of sauce to take out. Chef Boiardi would ask how many people would be eating the spaghetti and fill a glass milk bottle with the right amount of sauce. Since people asked why the spaghetti did not taste the same at home, Hector decided to include a package of his special blend of cheese with each bottle of sauce.

C-100

Then, "so there would be no difference from what people ate at the restaurant," Chef Boiardi decided to also include the uncooked spaghetti. The resulting complete packaged Italian Spaghetti Dinner was an immediate success.

Selling the new product to stores began to take up a great deal of Hector's time. He became concerned that this would negatively affect the restaurant so he asked a food distributor to handle sales. Before agreeing, the food distributor had Hector prepare his spaghetti dinner for the driver salesman in their truck garage. They liked it so much that Hector left the garage with an order that took two weeks to fill.

It was at this time that Hector Boiardi changed the spelling of the product to Boyardee. This was done because customers and even salesmen had difficulty pronouncing the Boiardi name. Mr. Boiardi always said that he made the change with sorrow, since "everyone is proud of his family name."

The Company continued its tremendous growth. During the 1930s, at the height of the Depression, Chef Boyardee Quality Foods outgrew three Cleveland plants.

By 1938, the Chef had converted an old silk mill in Milton, PA into the headquarters of Chef Boyardee. From there grocery stores throughout the country were supplied with the Chef's Dinners, Spaghetti Sauces, and Canned Pastas.

With the advent of World War II, the Milton plant was placed into the Service of the United States Government to prepare food for our troops. The Company became a major supplier of rations for the U.S. and Allied Armed Forces. Mr. Boiardi said that one of his greatest challenges was making carloads of ham and eggs into tasty field rations.

Soon after the war, Hector sold the company to American Home Products. He remained a valued advisor until his death at the age of 87 in 1985. The Chef's picture is still on each and every label that bears the Chef Boyardee name.

June 26, 1994
18B Old Hickory Dr. 2B
Albany, N.Y. 12204

Ross/Abbot Laboratories
Customer Service Dept.
11500 Rojan
El Paso, TX 79936

Dear Madam/Sir,

It is with hesitation that I send this letter, as it may seem a little out of the ordinary, but I feel I must.

Your product "Maximum Relief Clear Eyes" was used by myself to get rid of some problems with redness and itchy eyes I was having. What really got me to buy the product was the slogan "You Can Feel It Working". Well, I tried it and sure enough, I did feel it working. I felt it working quite a bit more than I expected.

Within minutes of having Clear Eyes in my eyes, the world became a surreal, bizarre acid dream. Colors whirled, peoples heads turned into different kinds of fruit, and my feet were stuck in cement. I spun and flew through a void of sparklers and smoke bombs until I woke up. It was the next day!

I'm just wondering if anyone else has ever reported these kind of "events" while on your product.

Very truly yours,

J.W. Fagan

(NO REPLY RECEIVED)

August 31, 1994
18B Old Hickory Dr. 2B
Albany, N.Y. 12204

Customer Service
FRUITOPIA
A CocaCola Foods Product
MINUTE MAID Division
Houston, Texas 77252

Dear Madam/Sir,

Well, it was another dead night here at the morgue (we
morticians pun a lot) and Bee was trying something new, called
FRUITOPIA. I just had to share the experience.

Without knowing Bee personally, you can't appreciate the
effect your beverage had. She's gregarious, confounding,
impoundable, overtaking, refraining, feinting, desultory and
particular. After sipping your drink for several minutes, she
became partisan, hypnotic, maligned, platonic, vapid, inclined and
fundamental.

Well, you can imagine our chagrin. She seemed quite taken by
the drink, and it's perfumous after effects. Her state of being
convinced myself, and a visiting pathologist from Akron, that she
truly enjoyed it. Tickled to death, as it were (sorry!).

I wish to inquire as to other flavors of Fruitopia. I'm not
big on mixed fruit, but would love to hear you have a Kiwi or
Papaya-based concoction. Would you, by any chance? I'd be
interested to know.

Very truly yours,

J.W. Fagan

Coca·Cola Foods
P.O. Box 2079
Houston, TX 77252-2079
Tel. 713-888-5000
A Division of The Coca-Cola Company

September 7, 1994

Mr. J.W. Fagan
18B Old Hickory Dr., 2B
Albany, NY 12204

Dear Mr. Fagan,

Thanks so much for taking the time to offer your kind words
about our Fruitopia Fruit Drinks.

It's nice to know our efforts are appreciated. We take a
great deal of pride in producing products that provide our
consumers with quality, flavor, value and convenience of
use. Consumer comments help guide us in our continuing
effort to win for our products the highest acceptance in the
marketplace.

Again, thanks for your words of praise. I hope that you will
remain a satisfied consumer of Coca-Cola Foods products for
many years to come and that you will recommend our products
to your friends.

Sincerely,

Rebecca L. Steckler

Rebecca L. Steckler
Representative
Consumer Information Center

09/07/94 6/1A 701
FRL/rls
Fruitopia Fruit Drinks
enc: Fruitopia Nutrition Chart
      Fruitopia Free Coupon
      3 Fruitopia 25 Cents Off

Minute Maid/Five Alive/Hi-C
Trademarks

PUBLISHERS
CLEARING
HOUSE
PRIZE PATROL

CARROLL ROTCHFORD
PORT WASHINGTON, NY 11050

Dear Friend:

Can I ask you to do me a favor? It will take just a few moments of your time, and it will be a big help to me.

You see, my boss Dave Sayer has just put me in charge of arranging the celebration party for our next Million Dollar winner. And with the winning number announcement just a few short weeks away, there's a lot of work for me to do and not a lot of time to do it.

> So here's the favor: since the winning number may be the one in this Bulletin, you could very well be the winner of $1,000,000.00 when you return your entry by the deadline. That's why I need your help <u>now</u> to begin preparations for what will definitely be a celebration to remember forever!

In the past our winners' celebrations have ranged from fancy dinners at a favorite restaurant to boisterous block parties with dozens of friends and neighbors in attendance. The choice is yours and, of course, we pick up the tab for all expenses.

So please help me by indicating below how you'd want to celebrate if you win. Then return the bottom portion of this letter with your entry form no later than July 28, 1994.

Thanks in advance for your help. I sure hope it's your house we pull up to in a few weeks when we award the next big Million Dollar prize!

Sincerely,

Carroll Rotchford
Carroll Rotchford
PCH Prize Patrol

------------------------------ Please fill out and return with your entry --------------------------------

Carroll, I'm delighted to help you arrange the winner's celebration! As the newest Million Dollar winner I'd prefer to celebrate at:

☐ My house with a few close friends and family members

☐ The block party to end all block parties

☐ My favorite restaurant (name below):

_____

I've also supplied a preliminary Celebration Guest List on the other side. I understand I will be free to make additions or deletions to this list once I am confirmed the winner.

Signature _____

CONFIDENTIAL

TO: Jim Fagan

FROM: Marcia Simon

SUBJECT: Prize Acceptance Affidavit

Jim Fagan,

As a recipient of this Bulletin, you are now in the enviable position of
being a potential winner of $10 MILLION.

Therefore, you have been assigned personal SuperPrize Number --
9121 6643 9114. It is now necessary to establish that you are indeed
fully qualified to accept the TEN MILLION DOLLAR prize should
9121 6643 9114 match the winning preselected number.

Enclosed herewith is the Prize Acceptance Affidavit generated in your
name. Please complete and return the original to us by July 28, 1994.
(Retain the copy for your records.) Once we receive this signed
Affidavit, SuperPrize Number 9121 6643 9114 will be registered. And
if it matches the winner, Jim Fagan will be our next multi-millionaire.

I must also tell you, Jim Fagan, that this may be the last invitation to
enter we can send you for some time. Unless you order this time or at
least write to us for more Bulletins, we may have to drop your name from
our mailing list because we just can't afford to send our Bulletins
regularly to folks who don't buy.

Rest assured that whether or not you're ordering, your Affidavit will be processed at once. So you should absolutely enter even if you don't order now.

But time is of the essence. We must have this Affidavit by July 28, 1994.
Once we receive it and reconcile the information with our records, you will
gain possession of SuperPrize Number 9121 6643 9114 and if it matches the
winning number, you'll win TEN MILLION DOLLARS.

Wait no longer. A pre-addressed reply envelope is enclosed for your
convenience. Please respond promptly but no later than July 28.

                          Sincerely,

                          Marcia Simon
                          Marcia Simon
                          Contest Director

C2739Wb

July 8, 1994
18B Old Hickory Dr. 2B
Albany, NY 12204

Ms. Carroll Rotchford
PCH Prize Patrol
Publishers Clearing House
Port Washington, N.Y. 11050

Dear Ms. Rotchford,

Your request for assistance in planning a winner's celebration was received and considered. It is, however, premature.

To date, I have not been notified I 've won any Prize worth celebrating about. The curiously enclosed fake affidavit (prepared similar to court guidelines, yet missing the venue and state regiments and a real notary public endorsement) was marked "confidential" and proceeded to threaten ME that if I didn't return the enclosed documents I may be excluded from further solicitation! Horrors!

Aside from the misleading and dubious statements made by your co-worker, Marcia Simon, in that mock affidavit, your own letter was admonishable. It takes real gall to blame participation in a cheesy marketing scam upon one's boss. Hey, if you got a problem with your boss or how your company does business, quit. There's plenty of rewarding work out there, especially in the government sector.

Do you realize, Carroll, the kind of damage a campaign like this does? Most of your victims are the elderly, who honestly believe that they have a chance at winning. They spend their meager savings - money squirreled away from childhood - to pay for magazines they never get, or are too blind from glaucoma to read. Think about it, these could be YOUR grandparents, Carroll.

I'm letting a few of my colleagues look over your "affidavit" for possible misrepresentation and false advertising. I'd suggest you, Carroll, find a more respectful and rewarding career. Believe me, there's no job satisfaction in hood-winking honest Americans. Especially those already battling the crippling effects of old age, mental retardation or loneliness.

Very truly yours,

J.W. Fagan

(NO REPLY RECEIVED)

August 30, 1994
18B Old Hickory Dr. 2B
Albany, N.Y. 12204

Customer Service
Continental Airlines
7300 World Way West
Los Angeles, CA 90009

Dear Madam/Sir,

What kind of business are your running?

I recently returned from a trip on one of your planes and I'm lucky to be alive. The trip was doomed from the start when a baggage door opened while we were taxiing for takeoff. I saw the bags come sliding out, and pointed that out to a rather surly "air hostess" who reluctantly put down her romance novel and called the pilot.

After retrieving the errant bags and tossing them back in, they took off. Never once apologizing for the inconvenience of almost causing a disaster!

If that wasn't enough, I nearly witnessed a woman choke to death on a hard roll. The hapless stewardess finally let a bystander with a brain Heimlich her to safety. The woman next to me never once stopped saying the rosary the whole trip. She must be a "frequent flyer".

Tell me, is this a rare occurrence? Or does this sound like an average flight?

Very truly yours,

J.W. Fagan

Continental

September 27, 1994

Continental Airlines, Inc.   Tel 713 987 6500
Customer Relations
Suite 500
3663 N Sam Houston Parkway E
Houston TX 77032

Mr. J. W. Fagan
18B Old Hickory Dr.
2B
Albany, NY 12204

Dear Mr. Fagan:

Thank you for contacting us about the difficulties you encountered with Continental Airlines. We certainly understand your concerns, and we sincerely apologize for the inconvenience you experienced, Mr. Fagan.

Continental Airlines is a customer-focused organization, and it is our primary objective to deliver quality service at all times. The situation you described is below our standards. I have forwarded your comments to our senior management staff so that corrective measures may be taken.

When we fail to provide our customers with the service they expect, we are most disappointed. It is more profitable to keep loyal customers than to advertise for new business. The airline industry is intensely competitive, and Continental will succeed only by offering excellent service.

Again, thank you for contacting us. Your comments are very important, and we appreciate your efforts in advising us. We hope you give us the opportunity to regain your confidence.

Sincerely,

M. Teague
Manager
Customer Relations

November 2, 1994
18B Old Hickory Dr. 2B
Albany, NY 12204

M. Teague
Manager
Customer Relations
Continental Airlines Inc
Suite 500
3663 N. Sam Houston Pkwy E.
Houston, TX 77032

Dear M,

Your response was warmly received and much appreciated. I can see from it that your company takes this customer service thing very seriously. Perhaps you could answer a quick question for me about something that's been gnawing at me for some time regarding airplanes.

With all the pollution in our environment, it seems to me that flushing human waste products into the open sky may be a little risky. Of course, it is biodegradable. That's not in contention. I'm sure you've heard the stories of frozen feces plummeting to earth and occasionally landing in populated areas, posing a serious "falling debris" hazard.

What I am curious about is what kind of ideas your company may have concerning in-flight waste containment for the future. Do you think Continental will move toward a "storage" or "Septic tank" type system in future years, or do they plan to stick with the tried and true "Flush and Fly" system?

Very truly yours,

J.W. Fagan

Continental

Continental Airlines, Inc.   Tel 713 987 6500
Customer Relations
Suite 500
3663 N Sam Houston Parkway E
Houston TX 77032

November 9, 1994

Mr. J.W. Fagan
18-B Old Hickory Drive, #2-B
Albany, NY 12204

Dear Mr. Fagan:

Thank you for your correspondence of November 2, 1994, to
Mike Teague, regarding Continental's waste containment
systems.

Mr. Fagan, in-flight waste containment is managed through
on board holding tanks. Each aircraft has the containment
tanks emptied at various times during the daily flight
schedule.

Again, thank you for bringing your concerns to our
attention, Mr. Fagan. We look forward to serving your
future travel needs.

Sincerely,

Patricia Fallows
Patricia Fallows
Manager
Customer Relations

September 6, 1994
18B Old Hickory Dr. 2B
Albany, N.Y. 12204

The Center for Sinus
 and Nasal Disease
475 Grand Ave
Englewood, New Jersey

Dear Madam/Sir,

To say that this letter is a plea for help would be an understatement.

Severe, rumbling, obstreperous and at times outright explosive snoring is a genetic feature of my family. My Uncle Charles, my Dad and my Aunt Sophie cavitate most vociferously in their sleep, to the point where spouses have been driven from the matrimonial bed. It has also been traced to the reason behind several pets which ran away, including an expensive Schnauzer named Pinky.

The first signs of this in my sleep showed up in college, where my girlfriend at the time broke up with me because of a stertor that she said (and I quote) "is so loud, there's no way you're not doing it on purpose just to bug me!" Well, not a big loss, but my roommate confirmed the raucous rale, and I fear for my future. Without going into an actual program, I just need to know one thing, is this genetic? And if so, am I condemned to richter-scale slumber for the remainder of my life?

I await your reply.

Very truly yours,

J.W. Fagan

THE **CENTER** FOR
SINUS & NASAL
DISEASE

436 THIRD AVENUE, NEW YORK, N.Y. 10016
476 GRAND AVENUE, ENGLEWOOD, N.J. 07631
(800) MD-SINUS

UNDERSTANDING SNORING

1. What is snoring?

Snoring occurs when the unsupported soft tissues in the mouth and throat -- the uvula, tongue, soft palate, tonsils and adenoids -- collapse into the airway. The muscles in these structures, which are unsupported by bone, relax during sleep and vibrate against each other. This creates the sound we know as snoring.

2. What causes snoring?

Snoring is usually caused by a combination of factors. They include:

- Throat tissue that is too large for its supporting structures
- overweight
- a soft palate or uvula that is too long
- a blocked nasal airway caused by a cold, sinusitis, allergy or deviated septum
- adenoid or tonsils in children

3. How can I reduce snoring?

There are a number of self-help measures that may reduce snoring. Individuals can:

- lose weight
- exercise regularly
- avoid tranquilizers including alcohol before bedtime
- elevate the head of bed
- sew a tennis ball into the back of their pajamas
- give their significant others ear plugs

4. How serious is snoring?

Very serious if it results in divorce! Seriously, heavy snoring may be an indication of a potentially life-threatening fatal condition called obstructive sleep apnea (OSA).

-more-

KENNETH F. GARAY, M.D., F.A.C.S. MEDICAL DIRECTOR
FRANK V. MIGNOGNA, M.D., F.A.C.S. CONSULTANT

November 8, 1994
18B Old Hickory Dr. 2B
Albany, NY 12204

Kenneth F. Garay, M.D.
Medical Director
The Center for Sinus
   and Nasal Disease
475 Grand Ave.
Englewood, New Jersey

   Dear Dr. Garay,

   Thank you for sending your report on "Understanding
Snoring". I have made copies and passed it around to my family
and friends.

   One question that has been raised in subsequent discussions
is regarding the "How Can I Reduce Snoring" section. One of the
many solutions offered in this segment is (and I quote) "sew a
tennis ball into the back of their pajamas". The suggestion which
follows this is equally puzzling; "give their significant others
ear plugs".

   Not only do these suggestions ring spurious, but hardly
sound like examples of modern medicine to me. What kind of
treatment do you folks involve your patients in, anyway?

   Could you explain?

                                        Very truly yours,

                                        J.W. Fagan

THE CENTER FOR SINUS & NASAL DISEASE

436 THIRD AVENUE, NEW YORK, N.Y. 10016
475 GRAND AVENUE, ENGLEWOOD, N.J. 07631
(800) MD-SINUS

February 24, 1995

J. W. Fagan
18B Old Hickory Drive, 2B
Albany, NY 12204

Dear J. W. Fagan,

My apologies for not responding sooner to your November inquiry regarding our mailing entitled "Understanding Snoring".

While I am unable to answer your questions because I am not of a medical background, it was suggested to me that I direct your attention to an excellent video on the topic of snoring put out by the American Academy of Otolaryngology. I do not know the specific title or production date, however, if you call the Academy's offices in Alexandria, VA I am sure they will be able to help. The most recent phone listing I have for the Academy is (703) 836-4444.

Once again, thank you for your interest.

Yours truly,

Raiani

Lisa Raiani, Office Manager

KENNETH F. GARAY, M.D., F.A.C.S. MEDICAL DIRECTOR
FRANK V. MIGNOGNA, M.D., F.A.C.S. CONSULTANT

October 9, 1994
18B Old Hickory Dr. 2B
Albany, NY 12204

John Kelly, General Manager
FLY 92
PO Box 12279
Albany, NY 12212

Dear Mr. Kelly,

I received your offer for a "Secret Salary" in the mail the
other day. Not to say that I wasn't tempted to sign up for such a
deal, but the tax implications finally scared me away.

Do you know, sir, the penalties imposed by the government
for undisclosed / unreported earnings? It's not a slap on the
butt, that's for sure. The Feds keep a watchful eye out for
schemes such as this, then swoop down to impose stiff and
sometimes crippling penalties for monkeying with "the system" by
paying undocumented workers. I'm surprised your station's
attorney did not catch this thing and nip it in the bud before
sending it out to the general public. You did present this to an
attorney before releasing, didn't you?

Don't worry about me, I don't plan on being the one to spill
the beans and spoil the fun. All I will do is offer a little
advice. A "secret salary" sounds like it would be nice, but so
does a "free lunch". And as I am sure you are aware, sir, there's
no such thing. Especially as far as the IRS is concerned.

Very truly yours,

J.W. Fagan

THE TRI-CITIES' ONLY HIT MUSIC STATION

October 19, 1994

J.W. Fagan
18B Old Hickory Drive 2B
Albany, NY 12204

Mr. Fagan,

I am writing in response to your letter dated October 9, 1994 regarding FLY92's current Secret Salary Contest.

To clarify the concept of the contest, FLY92 will award winners a cash prize. The prize can range anywhere from $92 to $736, depending on whether the person whose name is announced in subsequent hours calls the contest line within the allotted time frame. Persons participating in this contest do not actually become employees of WFLY, rather they become contest winners.

Under New York State tax law pertaining to contests and games of chance, any person winning over $600 must report that income. WFLY issues 1099 tax forms to any contestants meeting that criteria who have won any contest over the course of the year. WFLY also files all major contests with the State Attorney General's office in accordance with N.Y.S. law.

Please look over the enclosed contest rules which explain all details of this particular contest.

Thank you for you concern and for listening to Today's Hottest Hits on FLY92.

Sincerely,

Barbara A. Borini
Promotion Director

cc: John F. Kelly, General Manager

ALBANY BROADCASTING COMPANY INC.
4243 Albany Street   •   P.O. Box 12279   •   Albany, New York 12212   •   518-456-1144

October 9, 1994
18B Old Hickory Dr. 2B
Albany, NY 12204

President
VarTec Telecom, Inc.
3200 West Pleasant Run Road
Lancaster, Texas 75146

Dear Madam/Sir,

"E Pluribus Unum".

The print on a penny has been that way since its inception
in 1893 when our fore-founders started stamping out the little
copper ingots of dreams. Now, 100 years later, companies are
desecrating "little Abe" by using it to sell telephone plans.

Nothing gets me going like someone lifting their leg over a
symbol of America. Twenty years ago, a scam like this would have
called "Communist" or "Red" or "Pinko-neo-facist". Now it's
called "marketing".

Well I ain't buying into it. I plan to take my protest all
the way to the top. My desk holds letters from some very
influential corporate and political "movers and shakers", and I
plan to make them aware of this, starting with my good friend,
Mayor Jennings here in Albany. In all fairness, I will retard my
 action in allowance for a defensive rebuttal from your office,
dated no later than November 9, 1995.

Very truly yours,

J.W. Fagan

November 3, 1994

J.W. Fagen
18B Old Hickory Dr., 2B
Albany, NY 12204

Dear Mr. Fagen:

VarTec is in receipt of your correspondence dated October 9, 1994 and I am writing to you on behalf of A. Joe Mitchell, President of VarTec Telecom, Inc.

You note that VarTec is abusing the historical value of the United States penny by promoting it in its direct-mail piece. VarTec's intent is not to make a mockery of the penny but rather, to promote it for its monetary value. VarTec offers a program to both business and residential consumers that incorporates the ability to make certain qualifying telephone calls for one cent. VarTec includes a penny in its mailers to act as a reminder of the benefits of utilizing VarTec's long distance services

VarTec regrets that there is any misunderstanding of the Company's intent in marketing its long distance services. If you have further questions or comments regarding VarTec's service please contact the undersigned directly at 214-230-7200 or the Company's principal address.

Respectfully submitted,

A. Blevins
Consumer Analyst

VarTec Telecom, Inc.
3200 W. Pleasant Run Road
Lancaster, Texas 75146
(214) 230-7200
(214) 230-7299 Fax

November 9, 1994
18B Old Hickory Dr. 2B
Albany, NY 12204

A. Blevins
Consumer Analyst
VAR TEC TELECOM, INC.
3200 West Pleasant Run Road
Lancaster, Texas 75146

Dear A. Blevins,

Your timely reply crossed my desk as I was browsing through my collection of Campbell Soup labels. Talk about art.

Since writing to you, I have reconsidered my position on "the penny". The size of the National Dept dwarfs the once-honored penny, so that now it is little more than a joke. A gag. A grand, unintended jest.

Think about it. You cannot buy anything for a penny, not even one of those gum balls in the grocery store. In fact, I have been made aware of several groups lobbying Congress to have the penny discontinued as a minted monetary unit due to it's insignificance in the U.S. currency edifice.

Your company may need to reconsider it's position on the penny. In your attempt to "promote it's monetary value" as you say, you may come off looking outdated, old-fashioned and cheap. If you want to impress the general public, why not just slap a dollar bill on your direct-mail pieces? That would certainly impress me!

Let me know what you think.

Very truly yours,

J.W. Fagan

October 14, 1994
18B Old Hickory Dr. 2B
Albany, NY 12204

Donna Ferro
Consumer Relations Manager
SNAPPLE
1500 Hempstead TPKE
PO Box 9400
East Meadow, NY 11554-9400

Dear Ms. Ferro,

It's been some time since I heard from you regarding my
idea. I realize you folks get enourmous loads of correspondance
and an equally swollen assortment of wacky ideas. Mine, however,
was sincere.

As an American-Canadian (dual) Citizen, I know the
popularity of your product in both countries. My friends across
the 49th parallel see your commercials on the Yank networks and
love 'em. They are frustrated, however, because they cannot run
out and purchase the product which gives them such a warm and
fuzzy feeling over the media. They have to settle for some cheap
substitute.

So, I proposed to work with your company and devise and
good-will ambassadorship to bring SNAPPLE to Canada. A token of
not only good will, but of good business. Hey, Canadians are just
like us Americans (mostly, except in some areas of personal
hygene) and as you can see from your weekly sales figures,
Americans love SNAPPLE.

Please get back to me. I would like to know what's the
status of this idea with your "people". Thank you. Or as they say
in Canada, "Thanks, eh?".

Very truly yours,

J.W. Fagan

BEVERAGE CORP.

October 21, 1994

Mr. J.W. Fagan
18B Old Hickory Dr. 2B
Albany, NY 12204

Dear Mr. Fagan:

Thank you for writing to the Consumer Affairs Department at Snapple Beverage Corporation.

We wish to express our most sincere thanks for your favorable comments regarding Snapple beverages. We appreciate hearing from you and we are especially pleased to learn of your satisfaction.

Snapple is in Canada. We now have 3 distributors in that country.

Your continued patronage will be greatly appreciated.

Sincerely,

Donna Ferro
Representative
Consumer Affairs and Marketing

DJF/cl

0002723A

October 28, 1994
18B Old Hickory Dr. 2B
Albany, NY 12204

Donna Ferro
Consumer Relations Manager
SNAPPLE
1500 Hempstead TPKE
PO Box 9400
East Meadow, NY 11554-9400

Dear Ms. Ferro,

Thank you for your speedy, albeit disturbing, reply. You strike me as a dedicated employee.

I'm afraid you misunderstood my last letter to read that SNAPPLE was unavailable in Canada. As you pointed out, it is. The point I was trying to make was that Canadians are grievously unaware of the availability due to the "Americanization" of SNAPPLE (and rightly so - it is, after all, an American product). What you need here, Donna, is an angle to bring the Canadians "into the flock", as it were.

First, you blanket CBC and CTV networks with a few of your classic advertisements, maybe the "Mascot Tryouts" and the "Juvenile Delinquent" (where the kid gets a case of SNAPPLE delivered while in detention) episodes, which are both excellent. I'd skip the Ed Koch one, because they just wouldn't get it up there. The ironic humor is lost if you have no clue who Koch is (and they don't).

Anyways, then you slip in a few "Canadian" versions of your commercial styling (maybe a spot poking fun at the crusty Quebecers, or maybe one with a hockey theme) and voila! You'll have those Canucks sipping SNAPPLE faster than you can ship it up there.

I am currently unavailable to help out with a "goodwill tour" as I mentioned last time, though I will be up there for Christmas and plan to poke around and see if I can spark some interest for this concept. You may even want to think about adding some uniquely Canadian flavors, like "Canadian Goose Guava", or "Northwest Territory Medley". You may be able to do with juice what "Chunky Monkey" did for ice cream.

Let me know what you think.

Very truly yours,

J.W. Fagan

October 9, 1994
18B Old Hickory Dr. 2B
Albany, NY 12204

John Randall Drinko, President
Cleveland Institute of Electronics, Inc.
1776 East 17th Street
Cleveland, OH 44114

Dear Mr. Drinko,

I received your materials in the mail regarding a career in electronics. At one time, this literature would have been enthusiastically welcomed and hastily responded to. A recent situation has changed all that.

My good friend Sean (his nickname is "Sparks") O'Keefe was on a job site, and enlisted my brother (he will remain nameless for legal reasons) to assist in some light labor. Sean is a real electrician, my brother is not. He was holding a ladder for Sean while Sean was in a suspended ceiling doing some wiring. Boredom set in, and my brother wandered off to "take a break" with Sean still up in the ceiling. He started poking around the house (an unfinished single-family dwelling) and flicked a couple of light switches "because it was real dim in there". That's how Sean picked up the nickname "Sparks".

Thankfully, workman's compensation carried Sparks through what might have been a rough Christmas season and he's on the road to recovering the use of 80% of that hand. He has, however, developed a lisp that sounds strangely like an Irish accent.

The point of all this is, I don't feel the need to expose myself to similar peril. I'm sure your company offers fine training, but it's the people on the site WITHOUT training that scares me. Know what I mean?

Very truly yours,

J.W. Fagan

November 8, 1994

9409725303 ATI 42   MS 02
Mr. J.W. Fagan
18B Old Hickory Dr. 2B
Albany, NY 12204

Dear Mr. Fagan:

Thank you for your interest in the Cleveland Institute of Electronics. We are
the world leader in electronics home study and are pleased our courses are of
interest to you.

I am sorry to hear that you have decided not to enroll with us. If you
educational needs ever change, please feel free to contact me at any time.

I am enclosing a copy of our "Shocking Offer" as an option available to you.
You do not have to be enrolled at CIE to receive these introductory Electronic
and Electricity lesson materials. A one time payment of only $99.50 is all you
need to begin broadening your knowledge in the electronics field. This offer
is also completely transferable into most of our courses.

If you have any questions, please call me toll free at 1-800-243-6446,
extension 239. I hope to hear from you in the near future.

Sincerely,

Brad Bechtel
Admissions Counselor
Mail Sales Department
Extension 239

December 6, 1994
18B Old Hickory Dr. 2B
Albany, N.Y. 12204

Mrs. Anna
Psychic Reader
1149 Central Avenue
Colonie, New York

Dear Mrs. Anna,

I have a problem here and I'm hoping you can help. I saw
your ad in the paper and it said that you can tell the past,
present and future. All I ask is for some help here in the
present.

My girlfriend and I shared something very special until this
pretty-boy college kid came along wrecked the whole thing. She
was two-timing me for a while, but I always knew - I could see
that look in her lying eyes.

Now I need to fix them but good. First, I want to put some
bad karma on this guy, maybe have him get in a car accident or
flunk out of college or anything that will either 1) wreck his
good looks or 2) force him to take a job in a fast-food joint. The
way I see it, either of these "misfortunes" will send her
crawling right back to where she belongs.... with me!

You ad says you help on all problems and you can give peace
of mind. That's what I need. I'm on the road quite a lot, so I
need to know my woman is waiting for me with no other guy hanging
around causing disruptions. Let me know when we can meet so I can
give you this punk's name. I'm eager to get psychic on his ass!

Very truly yours,

J.W. Fagan

DEAR J.W. FAGAN.

I RECIVED YOUR LETTER AND UNDERSTAND YOUR PROBLUM. VERY WELL.

I CAN HELP YOU.

With THIS GIRL. AND HIM to YOU MUST CALL ME AS SOON AS YOU GET THIS LETTER. THER WILL BE A LOT MORE THINGS I MUST TELL YOU. IN PRIVET.

P.S. THIS IS MY FLYER. MY PHONE NUMBER IS ON FRONT. CALL ME. YOU NEED TO TALK TO ME.

Mrs. ANNA.

December 26, 1994
18B Old Hickory Dr. 2B
Albany, NY 12204

Ms. Loretta Strand
Assistant Vice President
Marketing
Publishers Clearing House
382 Channel Drive
Port Washington, NY 11050

Dear Ms. Strand,

Let's get real.

Never have I received such a solicitation! Kudos to you in your insightful wording of your letter. You basically say that I should feel guilty because here you are, offering me $10 million dollars, and I would buy a lousy magazine from you! Priceless!

Almost as good is that part where you say you don't want to pressure me, but you're going to stop sending me junkmail if I don't order something and I'm going to MISS hearing from you! You know what that sounds like? Like you're targeting a group of lonely, desperate folk.

Now I know you are just trying to make a buck like the next direct-mail-guy, but think about it. The retired people of our country survived two world wars, a great depression and the deaths of Elvis and Jim Henson. Now, you want to quicken their frail limbs to the cold, cold grave by building false hopes and threatening to halt their only source of communication with the outside world.... junk mail.

How do you sleep at night? You company is founded on scamming money from people who can least afford to be shammed.

Pleasant dreams.

Very truly yours,

J.W. Fagan

P.S. Incidently, your chances of winning from your company are about the same as meeting Michael Jackson in a quickie mart in Livingston, Montana at two a.m. sucking back a hoagie and humming Yanni tunes.

PUBLISHERS
CLEARING HOUSE
CUSTOMER SERVICE
382 CHANNEL DRIVE
PORT WASHINGTON, NEW YORK 11050

January 18, 1995

J W Fagan
18B Old Hickory Dr 2B
Albany, NY 12204

Dear J W Fagan:

You are right -- we are mistaken when we said you hadn't ordered any magazines from us before!

We hope you can understand that even at Publishers Clearing House, where our customer files are carefully maintained, mistakes like that can unfortunately occur once in a while. Our files may carry your name, address, and entry-order record more than once -- and in slightly different ways. The note you received was evidently based on one of those records and, as a result, was less accurate than you or I would wish.

Please accept our apologies for this mix up. We value your business -- and hope you'll continue to think of us as your #1 Magazine & Merchandise Source. And of course, we want you to keep entering our Sweeps for more chances to win giant cash prizes!

Rest assured that in the future, we'll do our best to see that all correspondence with you is letter perfect!

Cordially,

Robert H. Treller

Robert H. Treller, for
Publishers Clearing House

RHT dme
ihi

Over 35 Years of Excellence in Service...From Our House to Your House

TIME

THE WEEKLY NEWSMAGAZINE

Elizabeth Valk Long
Publisher

Dear Reader:

COULD YOU HELP US?

A few months ago you requested information from the Ontario Tourist
Board and we hope that you received the material you wanted and found it useful.
We are now conducting a survey to follow up and determine how satisfied you
were with the information we sent.

Your name was randomly selected from all those who responded to
receive this follow up questionnaire. Please be assured that your answers will be
kept strictly confidential when you respond. If for some reason you did not
receive your Ontario Tourism information and would like to, please add your
name to the form at the end of the questionnaire so that we may send you another
information packet.

We greatly appreciate the few moments of your time it should take to
complete the questionnaire and return it in the enclosed reply envelope.

Thank you!

Sincerely,

Elizabeth Valk Long
Publisher

P.S.   Please accept the enclosed $1 as a token of our appreciation for your
response.

January 30, 1994
810 Myrtle Ave #2
Albany, NY 12208

Elizabeth Valk Long
Publisher TIME
80 Cutter Mill Road
Suite 202
Great Neck, NY 11021

Dear Ms. Long,

I received your letter with much puzzlement and bewilderment, and would like to address a few issues before returning the questionnaire you sent.

First of all, what are you up to? The Ontario Tourist Board and TIME magazine are certainly strange bedfellows and I fail to see the connection not only between the them but between a Canadian office and an American media company. What probable connection could there be? Is TIME conducting an investigation into possible mis-appropriation of funds from within the Ontario Tourist Board? If so, is the Canadian Government involved in this, or is it merely a pilfering clerk from within the Board itself? I would be very interested in knowing what the story is, as I have close ties to the Liberal Party in Canada, and they pay well for tips on inter-governmental scandals.

I'm sure you'll understand why I will await your reply before submitting the survey. I will also hold the dollar bill in an escrow account in the interim, the interest of which can be divided evenly upon the resolution of this matter.

Sincerely,

J.W. Fagan

July 16, 1994
18B Old Hickory Dr. 2B
Albany, NY 12204

Elizabeth Valk Long
Publisher TIME
80 Cutter Mill Road
Suite 202
Great Neck, NY 11021

Dear Ms. Long,

Several months have passed, and I have not heard from you in regards to my letter of January 30, 1994. To refresh your memory, a copy of said letter is attached.

Basically, I'm following up on what was a puzzling letter from your office. As you can imagine, if you were to receive a similar letter, you too might start asking a few questions. Start poking here and there, lift a few rocks and see what scuttles out, so to speak.

Until now, I have been able to come up with a plausible theory as to why your office would be investigating the Ontario Tourist Board, and have refrained (up until now) from contacting the Canadian authorities. My patience, though, is wearing thin.

The check you sent for my services is still accruing interest in an escrow account, and will until I hear from you or a representative on this important matter.

Sincerely,

J.W. Fagan

TIME

Time Inc. Magazines

TIME
Time & Life Building
Rockefeller Center
New York, NY 10020

212-522-1212

August 5, 1994

J.W. Fagan
18B Old Hickory Drive 2B
Albany, NY 12204

Dear J.W. Fagan:

We have just received your letter of July 16 addressed to Elizabeth Valk Long, along with a copy of your January 30 letter. Sorry you have had to wait so long for a reply!

Let us assure you that the questionnaire you received was merely a market research study TIME was conducting for the Ontario Tourist Board who had advertised in TIME Magazine in 1993. The ad included an 800 # for readers to call and request additional information about travel in Ontario. As part of a follow-up survey, your name was randomly selected (along with several hundred others) from those who requested the travel brochures.

TIME occasionally conducts surveys like this as a service to our advertisers to help them in their marketing efforts; as do many other magazines. The purpose of this survey was to learn if the respondents were satisfied with the travel information they received and if they had taken, or planned to take a trip to Ontario. From the results the Ontario Tourist Board is able to assess the effectiveness of their advertising and promotion efforts.

Again, we are sorry it took so long for you to receive a response to your questions about our survey. Your original letter was sent to our research supplier along with the several hundred questionnaires returned by other survey participants and was not forwarded to us until now. Please use the dollar bill to help defray your mailing costs.

Sincerely,

For Elizabeth Valk Long
TIME Magazine

December 12, 1994
18 B Old Hickory Dr. 2B
Albany, N.Y. 12204

Customer Relations Manager
ADVIL
Whitehall Labs, Inc.
New York, NY 10017

Dear Madam/Sir,

Not since NoDoze have I encountered such an aptly-named product! Let me explain why!

I tried ADVIL while having an absolutely expounding headache, which is what I believe the stuff is for, right? Right. So there I was in my friends' medicine cabinet and I was hurting so I popped a couple of the little chicklets-of-relief and waited for the pounding to stop.

When I woke up I was soon aware that 48 hours had transpired and the weekend was now gone! The headache was, indeed gone, but with it two days which I can never get back. I missed Saturday Night live and Sunday Mass thanks to your little knock-out pill.

Have you had any other people report similar experiences? Is there a warning on the label that I failed to notice? Shouldn't you call the product 'Anvil' as opposed to 'Advil' to better describe the effects of taking it?

Very truly Yours,

J.W.Fagan

Whitehall-Robins
5 Giralda Farms
Madison, NJ 07940-0871
Telephone (201) 660-5500

January 3, 1995

J. W. Fagan
18 B Old Hickory Drive 2B
Albany, NY 12204

REFERENCE: ADVIL®

Dear J. W. Fagan:

Thank you for taking the time to contact us about Advil.

Before we can answer you questions we ask that you spend a few
moments to answer the enclosed questionnaire and return it to us
using the enclosed business-reply envelope labeled "ATTN: MEDICAL
AFFAIRS".

We value your interest in Whitehall-Robins products and we look
forward to receiving your response.

Sincerely,

Sandra Kwiatkowski, R.N.
Medical Affairs Department

SK:tjt
Enc.

January 11, 1995
18 B Old Hickory Dr. 2B
Albany, N.Y. 12204

Medical Affairs
Whitehall Labs
5 Giralda Farms
PO Box 871
Madison, NJ 07940-9955

Dear Madam/Sir,

I received your response to my inquiry and have filled
out the worksheet to the best of my knowledge.

To reiterate my dilemma let me simply say that I took
Advil and it knocked me cold for a long, long time. Not
surprisingly, I would like to know if this is a normal
feature of the drug, or if I happened upon maybe an "extra-
strength" dosage.

Please don't fear litigation or anything along those
lines. I'm seeking information only, so just give it to me
straight, and I will be on my way.

Very truly Yours,

J.W.Fagan

Fergan

WHITEHALL LABORATORIES
ADVERSE EXPERIENCE REPORT

WHITEHALL ROBINS

Product: Advil

Lot number on product: __?__   Expiration Date: __?__   Product size: YES

Reason for using the product: SPLITTING HEADACHE

Initials of the person who had the problem: J.F.   Age: 20's   Sex (M/F): M

Please describe in detail the problem that occurred when using the product: HAD A
HEADACHE. TOOK THREE ADVIL'S WITH WATER (can't
get them down without it). WOKE UP 2 day's later

What treatment was used for the problem? NO TREATMENT. JUST CURIOUS
WHY I GOT KNOCKED OUT FOR 2 DAYS !?!

Date product first used: 12/5/94   Date product last used: 14/5/94

What was the date the problem started? 12/5/94!

On average, how much of the product was used? ONCE. AFRAID TO TRY SINCE

What medicines were you taking at the time the problem occurred? NONE. I
STAY AWAY FROM DRUGS USUALLY. I BELIEVE IN THE
HEALING POWER OF COLD SHOWERS.

Are you allergic to anything? WORK. (JUST KIDDING.)

If yes, what is it and what happens when you are exposed to it? I ONCE WAS
BIT BY A CHIHUAHUA AND BROKE OUT.

Please add any other relevant medical information you feel is important: I HAVEN'T
BEEN IN A HOSPITAL SINCE BIRTH! NO BROKEN BONES, NOTHING.
HAVEN'T EVEN BEEN TO VISIT SIMEONE. I'M VERY HEALTHY!

What other medicines have you ever used for this problem? MASSAGE THERAPY,
LONG WALKS IN THE PARK, A FEW STIFF DRINKS.

Your cooperation in helping us to understand the problem you experienced is very much
appreciated. Kindly return the completed form using the enclosed pre-paid mailing label.

Whitehall-Robins
5 Giralda Farms
Madison, NJ 07940-0871
Telephone (201) 660-5500

April 28, 1995

Mr. or Mrs. J. W. Fagan
18 B Old Hickory Drive 2B
Albany, NY 12204

REFERENCE: ADVIL*

Dear Mr. or Mrs. Fagan:

We received the questionnaire you returned to us and thank you for taking the time to respond.

As you mentioned, there is not much information in this that can be analyzed for a proper response to you.

Yes, it would be unusual for three Advil tablets to cause you to be so-called "knocked out" for 15 hours. You have used Ibuprofen and Nuprin in the past and Advil is really the same medication.

We don't have a good explanation for this occurence but our best suggestion would be for you to consult your physician who is in the best position to understand your medical situation.

Sincerely,

Mina M. Bender, M.P.H., R.N.
Assistant Director
Medicial Affairs Department

MMB:tjt

September 19, 1994
18B Old Hickory Dr. 2B
Albany, NY 12204

Development Department
3-M Corporation
PO Box 3800
St. Paul, MN 55101

Dear Madam/Sir,

I am a small-time inventor with limited notoriety, and occasionally dabble in the culinary arts. While working in my "lab" last week, I stumbled upon what might be the "post-it note" idea of the decade. I call it, "Wacky Tape".

How many times have you wished you could find a tape with some "give" to it? Or, conversely, how often have you had to fiddle with tape rolls when they became "unmanageable". Well, no more, because Wacky Tape is stretchable, flexible, and does not adhere to skin! That's right!

Think of all the applications this tape could have in everyday life. I have. Why, the wrapping paper industry alone would benefit enormously, as would the packing and auto parts companies. Perhaps even the military could find a use. The possibilities are limited only by the imagination.

But I am a biased source. Perhaps you could "bring me down to earth" and give me an idea whether or not your company would be interested.

Very truly yours,

J.W. Fagan

P.S. I came to you guys first!

3M

September 28, 1994

J.W. Fagan
18B Old Hickory Dr. 2B
Albany, NY 12204

Dear Mr. Fagan:

Thank you for your letter in which you mention an idea which might be of interest to our company.

The enclosed ABOUT YOUR IDEA booklet explains the policy set by 3M for accepting ideas and also contains the Non-Confidential Idea Submission and Non-Confidential Information Questionnaire for the submission of your idea. Please complete these forms and return to our attention. We will then forward it to the appropriate division for their evaluation. As soon as we hear from them, we will let you know whether or not there is any interest on their behalf. Please keep in mind that it takes six weeks and sometimes longer for a proper evaluation.

Thank you for thinking of 3M with your idea.

Sincerely,

Marie Lee

Marie M. Lee
External Ideas Administrator

mml
Enc.

October 11, 1994
18B Old Hickory Dr. 2B
Albany, NY 12204

Marie M. Lee
External Ideas Administrator
3-M Corporation Technical Planning
3M Center
St. Paul, MN 55144-1000

Dear Marie,

Thanks very much for your speedy reply. From it, I can see you folks down there really stay on top of things.

You know, I have had occasion to work deals with other invention groups on prior ideas. You wouldn't believe the kind of run-around they gave me! One company wanted me to give them my secret ingrediants before agreeing to "take me on" as a client. Did they think I was born yesterday? Do I look a few fries short of a happy meal? I don't think so.

Admittedly, most "suits" just don't seem to know a good idea even when it slithers up to them and bites them on the shin. Glad to see you guys at 3M don't need a shot of poison to get them going.

Speaking of that, drop me a line when you get a free moment and let me know how the deal is progressing, would you? It would be good to hear from you.

Very truly yours,

J.W. Fagan

October 24, 1994

J.W. Fagan
18B Old Hickory Dr. 2B
Albany, NY 12204

Dear Mr. Fagan:

Thank you for your recent letter expressing concerns regarding your idea
submission.

To avoid conflicts of interest, 3M has found it necessary to adopt certain ground
rules for considering ideas submitted to 3M by outside persons. There are three
stages.

Stage 1: This is a preliminary stage in which we ask that you read this booklet
and realistically judge whether your idea could be of interest to 3M.

Stage 2: The procedure for Stage 2 depends on whether your idea is patented. If
your idea is unpatented (or if you have applied for a patent but it has not yet
issued) we ask you to complete our Non-Confidential Idea Submission
Agreement form found in the booklet (see details page 7 of booklet).

Stage 3: Evaluation of either your issued patent or your Non-Confidential Idea
Submission will take about six weeks and sometimes longer; at which time we will
write to tell you the results of our assessment.

If the rules for submitting your idea sound strict, it's only because we're trying not
to mislead you and because we want to protect our interests and yours. We
congratulate you for your creativity and thank you again for associating 3M with
new ideas.

Sincerely,

Marie Lee

Marie M. Lee
External Ideas Administrator

mml
Enc.

November 14, 1994
18B Old Hickory Dr. 2B
Albany, NY 12204

Customer Service Dept.
O'Doul's Division
Anheuser-Busch, Inc.
St. Louis, MO 63118

Dear Madam/Sir,

I direct a query to you regarding the product "O'Doul's Non-Alcoholic Beer".

While in the City (New York City, that is) on business, I was invited to imbibe with some senior executives in my company. Understandably, I was cautious in partaking in the mixing of alcohol and bosses, especially with my tendency to shoot off at the mouth when juiced. To play it safe , I decided to try your "O'Doul's" beer, which the bartender confided to me was non-alcoholic.

According to those present, after several rounds I grew "agitated and woozy" and appeared drunk. I apparently made numerous discolored and disrespectful asides about one manager's hairpiece, and a particularly stinging and libelous comment regarding the V.P.'s less-than-thin wife. None of this do I recall, but given my disposition, it is definitely possible.

Your product O'Doul's is advertised as a non-alcoholic brew. My experiences seem to prove the contrary results from drinking it. I am perplexed on how I became "drunk" from the product, unless the bottle was mislabelled and actually was REAL beer. Or, possibly careless storage on the part of bar owners led to an off-site fermentation process to occur. I don't know. All I know is that now I'm spending my mornings reading the classifieds and remain mere inches from going on a nice two-week bender to forget about the whole thing.

Before I do, I'd really like to know if your office can give me a hint as to what happened? Have you had reports of other accidental intoxications?

Very truly yours,

J.W. Fagan

(NO REPLY RECEIVED)

November 17, 1994
18B Old Hickory Dr. 2B
Albany, NY 12204

Consumer Service Office
Ralston Purina Company
Checkerboard Square
St Louis, MO 63164

Dear Madam/Sir,

For many months my canine has been on your "Fit and Trim"
diet, and I have yet to see any improvement in his condition.
Butch (that's my dog) remains a plump, lack-luster and unhealthy
specimen if I ever did see one.

It was his dull, wall-eyed gaze that drove me to purchase
your pet elixir with hopes of restoring that puppy-like
enthusiasm. Or at least get him to remain awake more than an hour
each day. Butch had no motivation to do little else but mope
around and watch t.v. all day like a bored housewife. Now I'm not
the picture of health myself, but I work all day and when I come
home I like a stiff hi-ball and a few mindless television
programs like anybody else. But what's Butch's excuse? After all,
it's a dog's life, right?

So I started him on that Fit and Trim deal and dumped the
Fancy Feast stuff he used to get in the garbage. Also, I tie his
leash to the treadmill with the setting on "jog" and made him
stay on it for an hour once a day. Damn if the pooch still has no
gumption or even the glint of life in his eyes. All this Fit and
Trim thing has done is made it so he growls if I come near him
with the leash. Also, he now goes through the garbage regularly
which I have to clean up. Yeeech.

I'm a little out of my league here. You guys are the
experts, so please tell me what's up? What am I doing wrong?

Very truly yours,

J.W. Fagan

 **Ralston Purina Company**

Grocery Products Group
Office of Consumer Affairs

December 5, 1994

Mr. J.W. Fagan
18-B Old Hickory Drive, 2-B
Albany, NY 12204

Dear Mr. Fagan:

Thank you for contacting us concerning Purina Fit & Trim brand Adult
dog food. We regret that you are dissatisfied with the results of this
product.

There are a lot of factors which determine whether a dog will loose
weight on Fit & Trim. What was the dog eating before? Does the dog
get any table or human food? Is the dog getting any exercise? What
breed of dog is it and what is his/her ideal weight? Without answers
to these questions, it is hard to determine why your dog has not lost
weight.

Also, you mention that your dog growls every time you go near with the
leash and feel that this may be attributed to the Fit & Trim. On the
other hand, it could be that the dog does not like the workout on the
treadmill.

We tried to contact you by phone to discuss this with you but were
unable to obtain a telephone number for you. We would certainly be
happy to discuss our questions and any additional questions you may
have. Please give us a call at 1-800-778-7462 and we will be happy to
discuss this matter with you.

We are most anxious to restore your confidence in our products. Thus,
we hope you will use the enclosed complimentary coupons the next time
you go shopping. We feel sure your next purchase will be to your
satisfaction.

Thank you for buying Ralston Purina products.

Sincerely,

Linda Riley
Consumer Representative

**FROM THE DESK OF
WILLIAM AUSTIN**

AMERICAN FAMILY PUBLISHERS
MAIL CONTROL BUREAU

ATTENTION:

I have been asked to advise you of an urgent matter: YOUR MAILING PRIVILEGES WITH US MAY BE IN SERIOUS DANGER.

If your group status is either 0740, 0840, 0940 or 1040, that places you in STATUS ALERT. This means you are among a group of people on our mailing list who may be dropped.

CHECK RED BOX ON ADDRESS LABEL
FOR YOUR CURRENT GROUP STATUS.

Because of rising costs, we will be forced to cut back on the number of people on our regular mailing list. We guarantee that our good customers will continue to hear from us. They are the only ones who will definitely receive all of our best offerings, including the exciting news and opportunities ahead.

Unless you place an order or write to stay on our list, YOU MAY BE FORFEITING ANY RIGHTS TO FUTURE MAILINGS. I urge you to act at once and UPGRADE your group status to PRIORITY by ORDERING TODAY!

William Austin

**William Austin
for American Family Publishers**

44D11
©1984 AFP

EP

**IMPORTANT: IF ORDERING, PUNCH OUT 'FORFEIT' STAMP
ON REPLY ENVELOPE FLAP FOR IMMEDIATE PRIORITY UPGRADE!**

September 1, 1994
18B Old Hickory Dr. 2B
Albany, N.Y. 12204

Mr. William Austin
c/o American Family Publishers
P.O. Box 62143
Tampa, Fla 62143-2143

Dear Bill,

Received your urgent note regarding my mailing privileges and
thought I ought to reply. It sounded serious.

Sorry to hear you are experiencing cash-flow problems, but
these are fiscally troubled times. I too have been forced to drop
a few employees in order to keep the profit margin up, so I know
where you're coming from. However, I think I can help out.

Your letter states that, "Unless you place an order or write
to stay on our list, YOU MAY BE FORFEITING ANY RIGHTS TO FUTURE
MAILINGS!" Unless I am mistaken, that means if you don't hear from
me in the form of an order or address confirmation, you may stop
sending me material. WELL, HALLELUJAH!!!!!!!!! I've been trying to
"lose my mailing privileges" for five years now! You could have
saved yourself time and money by doing this sooner, as far as I'm
concerned.

Don't worry, you shall remain on my Christmas Yam Gift List
for 1994, and can expect to receive it around the same time as the
one came last year. Give my regards to your wife.

                                        Very truly yours,

                                        J.W. Fagan

(NO REPLY RECEIVED)

October 15, 1994
18B Old Hickory Dr. 2B
Albany, NY 12204

Customer Service
Wendy's Restaurants of Canada, Inc.
6715 Airport Road, Suite 301
Mississauga, Ontario L4V 1X2
CANADA

Dear Madam/Sir,

I have just returned from a visit your little corner of the
World (Ontario) and it's good to be back. Why? Because you folks
are crazy.

While in a Wendy's up there, I experienced a truly unique
dining experience. The service at the counter was as good as
could be expected (bored, underpaid employees in funny uniforms)
and the food was mostly warm. It was the "ambiance" that caught
me unawares. A man sitting next to us paused from eating, a
blanched look on his face. He muttered something unintelligible,
then vomited on my companion.

The staff found the situation too amusing to be of any
assistance. My cries for a towel or large amounts of paper
products were met by responses of "take her outside and hose her
off first" and "don't bring her in the washroom, you'll make a
mess in there".

This was certainly an unpleasant and uncomfortable
situation, compounded by inept, uncaring employees. Is this how
your staff is trained? Or was this an "isolated, curious
incident" and not worthy of a response?

Very truly yours,

J W Fagan

November 8, 1994

Mr. J. W. Fagan
18B Old Hickory Dr. 2B
Albany, NY
12204

Dear Mr.Fagan:

Thank you for your comments informing us of an unpleasant experience that happened at one of our restaurants. We always appreciate hearing from our customers and are sorry for the undue frustration you experienced.

Customer service is Wendy's first priority. Keeping you satisfied is the primary responsibility of our restaurant personnel. Firstly, I would like to say sorry about the quality of the food and the service that you received at this particular location. This is not the norm at any of our locations. Secondly, rude treatment of a customer or inappropriate behavior is a mistake that none of our people can afford to make. Without customers, we simply would not be in business.

Unfortunately, you did not mentioned in your letter the location that you visited on that day. Therefore, at this time we are unable to deal with the the restaurant in question to ensure that an incident such as this doesn't happen again. If you could at your convenience, please let us know which of our location you were at.

Mr. Fagan, sorry for any inconvenience that this may have caused and thank you for bringing it to our attention.

Best regards,

Wendy's Restaurants of Canada

Rose DeLuca
Customer Service

December 11, 1994
18B Old Hickory Dr. 2B
Albany, NY 12204

Mr. Orville Redenbacher
Hunt-Wesson, Inc.
PO Box 4800
Fullerton, CA 92634

Dear Mr. Redenbacher,

It is an honor to attempt correspondence with you, sir.

I am a long-time eater of your fluffy corn product and have one minor complaint. Do you know when you eat popcorn how the kernel shell   gets stuck in the space between the gums and your teeth? I hate that!

Do you have a research team you can assign to look into this? I'd be beside myself if you folks could come up with something. How about it?

Also, are the commercials real? Did you win all those ribbons and medals for popcorn? Really?

Very truly yours,

J.W. Fagan

HUNT WESSON, INC.
P.O. Box 4800
Fullerton, CA 92634-4800
714 680-1431

January 16, 1995

Mr. J. Fagan
18B Old Hickory Dr., #2B
Albany, NY 12204

Dear Mr. Fagan:

I am writing in response to your inquiry regarding Orville Redenbacher's Popping Corn.

The hull, or the part that gets stuck between your teeth, is the outer covering of the popcorn kernel. It is necessary to retain the proper moisture level in the corn. Popcorn that pops more fully pops the hulls off however, it's not possible to make a hulless popping corn.

Thank you for your interest.

Sincerely,

Jennifer Clark

Jennifer C. Clark
Manager
Consumer Communications

a ConAgra Company

January 24, 1995
18B Old Hickory Dr. 2B
Albany, NY 12204

Jennifer C. Clark
Hunt Wesson, Inc.
PO Box 4800
Fullerton, CA 92634-4800

Dear Ms. Clark,

Thank you for the information on those annoying but necessary popcorn hulls. I guess like most things life, you have to take the lumps to enjoy the porridge.

While discussing the theory of the hull with my popcorn-learned roommate, Leigh, the idea was put on the table that perhaps something could be done to make those hulls more functional. Being a scientist of some renown, Leigh has tackled many conundrums and had an interesting conjecture on this hull thing.

He suggests using a form of polymer which, under heat, would break down and separate from the corn kernel. The polymer then can either evaporate (my idea) or flow to the bottom of the kernel pile, where it would cool after removal from the heat source and form a kind of bowl under the now popped corn. The last part seemed kind of out-there to me, but Leigh knows a thing or two about science and what not, and assures me it is entirely viable.

Let me know what you think. If you like the idea maybe you can give Leigh some money to develop this polymer for you, as he occasionally does freelance work (minus a small finders fee for me, of course). Also, in my previous letter I wondered if Mr. Redenbacher had really won all those ribbons he wears in his commercials for his popcorn. I'd really like to know the answer to this, for it is true I would find it astounding and imperturbable.

On a personal note, I hope you are keeping out of the way of the mud slides and enjoying your balmy winter weather you folks are having out there right now. Just to make you feel good, it's whippin' cold out here in the East. I guess it all goes back to what I was saying about taking the bad with the good, eh?

Very truly yours,

J.W. Fagan

January 2, 1995
18B Old Hickory Dr. 2B
Albany, NY 12204

Meditation Manager
The Albany Kripalu Yoga Center
1698 Central Avenue
Albany, New York

Dear Madam/Sir,

I am a very busy man, but I want to take a moment to inquire about yoga. Your ad in the newspaper caught my eye.

Although my business florishes like a flower in the sun, my health is more like a broken watch. I've been checked out by a few doctors, and the universal cry has been "EXERCISE!". Well, to be honest, the most exercise I get is walking from my house to the limo and from the limo into my building. I start panting just thinking about working out, and the sweat breaks out when I watch sporting events on tv. I've gone through a six-pack of trainers and even more diets. What I need is something different.

My biggest concern about yoga is it's stigma of being a drug-related, psycadellic-type work out. Drugs and me don't mix, except for beer, so I can't be dropping acid or anything. At this point, I'll give anything a shot because my doctors are pleading for me to do something. But I don't go for anything too out far out there.

I'd appreciate it if you could shoot me a note on this.

Very truly yours,

J.W. Fagan

THE ALBANY
KRIPALU YOGA CENTER
A Special Place For Wellness and Learning   1698 Central Ave. Albany, NY 12205 (518) 869-7990

1/18/95

Dear Mr. Fagan

Just a brief note to respond to your inquiry. Enclosed is our brochure of class/workshop offerings

Yoga has never, or will never, promote the use of drugs of any kind. We do not encourage the use of any artificial stimulants, it is contrary to the philosophy.

Please read the brochure and call us if you'd like to receive our spring issue for a listing of classes offered in '95.

I would love to speak with you by phone at your convience. Please call to set up a phone meeting

Best wishes for a healthy New Year!

Vanditar (Kate)

January 3, 1995
18B Old Hickory Dr. 2B
Albany, NY 12204

U.S. Postmaster GMS
U.S. Postal Service
Albany, New York 12288

Dear Madam/Sir,

Like most Americans, I noticed you recently raised the
postal rate. Most of the press on this event has been mixed, and
so I'm hoping you shed some light on the increase.

Mostly, I'd like to be reassured this inflation in stamp
prices will also lead to a better postal service. In other words,
does this bump in fees mean that the authorities will no longer
be finding dumpsters full of mail? Will the additional revenue be
passed along to the hard-working postal workers, so that they
won't be disgruntled and bring bags of mail to their apartments?

A thought I had is that they should divert some money to a
slush fund and throw the mail carriers and management a party
once a month, a kind of let-your-hair-down bowling and beer blast
that could relieve a lot of tensions and build some spirit. That
kind of activity has been found to work wonders for firemen, and
you know the kind of stress they're under!

I look forward to hearing from you.

Very truly yours,

J.W. Fagan

POSTMASTER
ALBANY POST OFFICE

UNITED STATES
POSTAL SERVICE

January 12, 1995

J.W. Fagan
18B Old Hickory Dr. 2B
Albany NY 12204-1133

Dear Mr. Fagan:

Thank you for your letter regarding the recent rate increase. I can certainly understand your concerns and appreciate the opportunity to address them.

As the rate of inflation rises, so does the cost of operating a business. The Postal Service has operating expenses just like everyone else. The Postal Service is not subsidized by your tax dollars, therefore, our operating expenses must be covered by moneys taken in through the sale of stamps and services. The Postal Service has held rates stable for a record four years. This rate increase is, in fact, lower than the rate of inflation for this same time period. Even at 32 cents, a first-class stamp is among America's best buys. Compare it with Japan's 81 cents or Germany's 65 cents.

Will the new rate lead to a better Postal Service? This 3 cent rate increase does not reflect upon the level of service you receive -- any more than an increase in prices will get you more gas to a gallon or more bites to the candy bar. But I do hear your concern.

We're working hard every day to improve service quality. Last year we achieved record customer satisfaction as measured by an independent system, and we're committed to building on that accomplishment. Today, 85% of the American public feel their service is "excellent, very good or good" according to the latest survey conducted by Opinion Research Corp.

The reference you make to "finding dumpsters full of mail" is isolated and not reflective of the type of service you receive from the over 750,000 employees who provide service to over 123 million households daily.

Employee Commitment is one of three major goals of the Postal Service and we expend a great deal of our resources to that goal. Some of which include: Excellent pay supplemented by excellent family benefits; Employee Involvement Committees consisting of employees and managers working together for quality of work life; Several communication tools; Recognition Awards such as "Certificates of Appreciation" and "Special Achievement Awards" which can be supplemented with cash; Employee Assistance Programs dedicated to providing employees help with their personal problems; Employee Crises Teams dedicated to recognizing and relieving stressful situations for our employees. Of course, we also encourage all managers to provide individual recognition and praise. These managers often reward their employees with "coffee and bagels", pizza's for lunch, etc.

While you are generous with your good intentions, most Americans -- and certainly our legislators -- would not tolerate our using Postal funds to give our employees "a party" or "beer blast". We do encourage, however, and participate in such endeavors when they are funded by employees and their unions and look for advertising opportunities that have benefits we can share with our employees.

I appreciate your concern for our employees welfare and hope that I have addressed your concern regarding customer service as it relates to the rate increase.

Thank you for writing.

Most sincerely,

R.L. Poulin, Sr.
Postmaster

February 7, 1995
18 B Old Hickory Dr. 2B
Albany, N.Y. 12204

Consumer Inquiries
LifeSavers Division
PO Box 41
Winston-Salem, NC 27102

RE: Carefree Gum

Dear Madam/Sir,

While happily chewing a stick of your CAREFREE gum, I had
occasion to notice the warning you placed modestly on the
confection. In bright white it reads; "USE OF THIS PRODUCT MAY BE
HAZARDOUS TO YOUR HEALTH. THIS PRODUCT CONTAINS SACCHARIN, WHICH
HAS BEEN DETERMINED TO CAUSE CANCER IN LABORATORY ANIMALS."

You mean to tell me I have been enjoying a product with a
name like "Carefree" that could give me a tumor the size of a
eggplant? I hardly call that Carefree! That would be like calling
a chocolate bar that gave you leukemia "Happiness".

How long do I have to live? I chew this stuff a lot and I'd
like to find out how much time I will have to put my affairs in
order before I check out of this brainless world. Please respond
quickly, as a "carefree" response would eat up what little time I
have remaining.

Very truly yours,

J.W.Fagan

 **Planters LifeSavers Company**

Winston-Salem, NC 27102
(910) 741-2000

February 16, 1995

Mr. J. W. Fagan
18-B Old Hickory Drive #2B
Albany, NY 1220

Dear Mr. Fagan

Thank you for contacting Planters LifeSavers concerning CARE*FREE
Sugarless Gum.

In response to your concerns/questions on the use of saccharin:

- Saccharin is approved for use by the U. S. Food and Drug
   Administration.

- Saccharin is used in our products and labeled in accordance with
   federal law. It is one of the most studied ingredients in the food
   supply chain and has been evaluated extensively in many species of
   animals and in human epidemiologic studies. The only evidence of
   adverse health effect was found in one species of male rats fed very
   high doses of saccharin. Extensive research indicates that saccharin
   does not pose a health risk to humans.

- Market research on our products with saccharin showed that consumers
   preferred the superior taste provided by saccharin over other sugar
   substitutes.

Before a new product is marketed, or an established product
reformulated, Planters LifeSavers attempts to determine the preferences
of our consumers. Market research surveys and taste tests are conducted
to help us make those decisions. Our results show that consumers
preferred the taste provided by saccharin.

I hope this letter answers your questions about saccharin and our use
of it in our products.

Thank you again for contacting us.

Sincerely,

Lynora Essic
Lynora G. Essic
Consumer Information Services

LGE/bso

Enclosure

0191275A

February 11, 1995
18B Old Hickory Dr. 2B
Albany, NY 12204

J.Patrick Miller
National Association of Rocketry
PO Box 177
Altoona, WI 54720

Dear Mr. Miller,

I can't say how cool it is that there is a National club for
rocket heads like me! I almost freaked when I got your address.

I've gotten hours of enjoyment combining my two loves,
rocketry and cinematography. What I do is set up the video camera
and film the launchings. I make a whole set, with a launch pad
and little workers all around and sometimes there are premature
firings of the rocket and several workers get burned.

My skills have gotten so good I can put a target on the barn
almost 100 yards away and hit it with a single stage engine fired
at an angle. My cousin climbs up in the trees and hangs paper
plates across the field and I try to hit those too.

My question is are there competitions I could enter for
this? Also, do you have a newsletter with maybe hints on how to
get more power out an engine? My mom won't let me buy the really
big ones yet.

I'm sure you have a big club, so I'm hoping you can help.

                                        Very truly yours,

                                        J.W. Fagan

National Association of Rocketry

Post Office Box 177
Altoona WI 54720
(715) 832-1946
(800) 262-4872

JW Fagan
18 B Old Hickory Drive - 2B
Albany, NY   12204

Dear JW,

While I am excited to hear that you have a love of rocketry, I cannot endorse your
dangerous activities. There are no competitions for the activities you described, as
rocket engines are not designed to be used to shoot vertically at targets.

I would suggest greater supervision on the part of your parents and perhaps a
talking-to on the dangers of miss-use of these engines. You are an accident waiting
to happen.

Sincerely Yours,

John Brennen

JMB:las

February 15, 1995
18 B Old Hickory Dr. 2B
Albany, N.Y. 12204

Customer Service
Pillsbury Company
2866 Pillsbury Center
Minneapolis, MN 55402

Re: Green Giant Products

     Dear Madam/Sir,

     When you think of Green Giant, images of a hulk-like figure
stomping down the valley, sending farmers running for the trees
comes to mind. I for one have always enjoyed the adventures of
the gentle jade homesteader, but recently a friend of mine
commented on one of the ads and raised some valid points which I
wish to address here.

     First of all, where did the Jolly Green come from? Is he
related to the giant of "Jack and the Beanstalk" lore? If so,
does he live in the clouds and have a chicken laying golden eggs?

     Secondly, Sprout never seems t get any bigger. His name
suggests that he has the potential to "grow" into something
bigger than a mere "sprout". If so, what? And does he attend
classes at a local school? If he does, is he leaning toward the
marketing and sales side of the trade, or will he be a Giant,
like Jolly Green?

     In a symbolic way, I'm sure the Jolly Green Giant is meant
to represent a strong, healthy figure for the company as well
keep the competition in line with the subliminal threat of being
stepped on by the huge, green foot. Unfortunately the running
farmers and the symbolism of green can be taken in other ways as
well. Green for the avarice of the corporation, and the
scattering farmers the small business operator who goes down due
to monopoly of the resources and markets by the Green Giant
Corporation.

     Please dispel these misinterpretations and put my friend in
his place!
                         Very truly yours,

                         J.W.Pagan

The Pillsbury Company
Consumer Relations
P.O. Box 550
Minneapolis, MN 55440
U.S.: 1-800-767-4466
Canada: 1-800-767-5350

March 3, 1995

J.W. Fagan
18B Old Hickory Dr., Apt. 2B
Albany, NY 12204

Dear J.W. Fagan:

The Jolly Green Giant® and Little Green Sprout™ asked me to write
to you. They enjoy hearing from good friends like you.

We hope the enclosed information will be helpful and that you will
continue to use and enjoy our products.

Sincerely,

Sally Selby

Sally Selby
Vice President, Consumer Relations

95030201556
9503030001

HOW THE GREEN GIANT WAS BORN

How did the Green Giant trademark originate?

The story goes way back to 1903 when a small group of adventurous individuals pooled their life savings and started a corn cannery called the Minnesota Valley Canning Company. The Company jogged along until the early 1920's when it made a significant breakthrough in seed development: a new variety of peas. What distinguished them from what was generally available in the U.S. was that they were very large in size, yet remained very tender in texture. The code name for the research people who worked on the project was "Green Giant" - a simple description of the product. They were "green" in color and "giant" in size.

Ward Cosgrove, whose father started the company, was general manager of the small firm at the time. Green Giant Brand Peas were first marketed in 1924, simply as a brand with no trademark in sight. In 1926 Ward Cosgrove suggested that if they were called "Green Giant" peas, why not create a giant as a trademark. So the first Giant was born.

But he wasn't green and hardly a giant in stature. He looked more like a direct link with Neanderthal man. This was the first step in the development of the Green Giant trademark.

In 1928, another bold step: If he was called the Green Giant, then why not make him green in color? So, in that year, he adopted the healthy, green hue he bears to this day. This might seem like a logical step to us now, but in its time it must have been a revolutionary creative decision.

The same year another giant arrived on the scene and put an indelible stamp on the personality of the Green Giant. The Minnesota Valley advertising agency at the time was the Erwin Wasy Company, with a young man by the name of Leo Burnett as copy supervisor. In the early 1930's, a procession of account executives carried black bags full of advertising campaigns to LeSueur, Minnesota, the home town of the Minnesota Valley Canning Company. One day, in a conversation with the agency president, Ward Cosgrove remarked: "I wish you'd let that little copywriter of yours bring the ads up. He gets more accomplished than anyone else." So Leo Burnett became responsible for the creative development of the Green Giant.

It was Leo who was responsible for making the Green Giant "Jolly." Some years ago, Leo was quoted in these words: "I was serving as both president and copy chief of the agency when a proof of a *Ladies' Home Journal* ad came across my desk. Because it was so alliterative and just for the heck of it, I inserted the word, 'jolly' in the ad about to go to press. Green Giant liked it and it has remained importantly in the Green Giant vocabulary ever since."

It remained for television, however, to provide the now famous "Ho Ho Ho." Bob Noel, Executive Vice President and Creative Director at Burnett, and the originator of the "Valley of the Jolly Green Giant" television campaign, inserted the thundering "Ho Ho Ho" almost as an afterthought in the early steps of developing the campaign. It was an immediate hit with the public.

In the years since the Green Giant has appeared as a brand, he has changed considerably in appearance. The Giant on today's labels has moved a long way from the caveman version of the mid-1920's. He will continue to evolve.

February 16, 1995
18 B Old Hickory Dr. 2B
Albany, N.Y. 12204

Helen Johnson
S.C. Johnson & Son
Racine, WI 53403

Re: EDGE (with Aloe)

Dear Ms. Johnson,

As a part-time mechanical engineer of minor repute, lubricants are my hobby. Your shaving cream product, EDGE (with Aloe) has properties you may not be aware of, and I thought you should know about what I have found.

While changing the CV joint on an '84 Subaru, my lack of a white grease became appallingly apparent. My neglect to prepare for the job was more than a little embarrassing, as with the car apart I was hardly in the position to go out for a drive and get some more. I rummaged through the garage in hopes of finding a substitute and the only thing I found was a can of your shaving foam. If I was in a cartoon you would have seen a light bulb appear over my head for at that moment I had a revelation.

With generous helpings I lathered up the boot joint and affected area. After re-packing the fitting, away I went! It worked great! No squeaks squeals or creaks whatsoever.

What's up with that? Any clues as to why it's such a good axle grease? Would the Aloe have anything to do with it? Perhaps you should consider putting out an "industrial strength" EDGE for AUTO'S or change the name altogether and market it as an automotive grease. Maybe you could call it "Lubricant with Aloe".

Very truly yours,

J.W.Fagan

SC Johnson WAX

S.C. Johnson & Son, Inc.
1525 Howe Street
Racine, WI 53403-5011
Phone: (414) 631-2000

March 2, 1995

Mr. J. W. Fagan
18 B Old Hickory Drive
2 B
Albany, NY 12204

Dear Mr. Fagan:

Thank you for contacting us about EDGE Shaving Gel. Compliments are always nice to receive. Your comments will be shared with appropriate personnel in our company.

We'd like you to know that EDGE Shaving Gel has been formulated, designed and tested only for those uses described on the label. We hope you'll understand that we are unable to recommend using it the way you described.

The guiding philosophy of SC Johnson Wax has always been to market products that are superior to those of our competitors. When our products are used according to label directions, we hope our high standards will be quickly recognized by consumers.

To show our appreciation, some coupons are enclosed. If we can be of help in the future, feel free to contact us again.

Sincerely,

Nina M. McGee
Consumer Specialist

File reference: 1506659

March 28, 1995
18 B Old Hickory Dr. 2B
Albany, N.Y. 12204

Mr. Robert B. Reich
Secretary of Labor
Department of Labor
200 Constitutional Avenue
Washington, DC 20210

Dear Mr. Reich,

Greetings and salutations, Mr. Secretary. I hope this note finds you enjoying your appointed status and the wild "Washington Scene". I'm not one for politics and in fact can't stand for talking about such things. When there's a job to be done, I just do it. But I digress.

My question to you is regarding work. I have a few beefs with the kind of stuff that goes on at my workplace and I hope you can do something about it.

The boss is a bloated, ubiquitous, know-it-all blow-hard that scoffs at child labor laws and laughs heartily at the "employees must wash hands" sign in the bathroom. He works us for seven days straight without a day off and then says we are "not committed to providing quality tacos" when we try and ask for a day off. Mr. Reich, I am one of the hardest-working gringo burrito preparer this side of the Mexican border. I try hard and for my efforts what do I get? I'll tell you what, I get assigned to rummaging through the garbage bins for re-usable drinking cups and food wrappers to cut supply costs.

Something has to be done! My boss cuts more corners than a New York cab driver, and somebody's going to get hurt. Just last week a guy lost the tip of a finger in the lettuce shredder and all he received for his trouble was an extended break and a free burrito.

Take it from me, it's hard to hold your head high in a place like this. Can you offer any help?

Very truly yours,

J.W.Fagan

U.S. Department of Labor   Employment Standards Administration
Wage and Hour Division
Washington, D.C. 20210

APR 1 4 1995

J. W. Fagan
18 B Hickory Drive, 2B
Albany, New York 12204

Dear Mr. or Ms. Fagan:

This is in response to your letter addressed to Secretary of
Labor Reich concerning your employment at a food service
establishment. Your letter has been referred to this office for
a reply.

The Wage and Hour Division of the U. S. Department of Labor
administers and enforces the Fair Labor Standards Act (FLSA), the
Federal law of most general application to minimum wages, hours
of work, and child labor. Currently, the minimum wage is $4.25
per hour. Under the child labor provisions of FLSA, 16 is the
basic minimum age for employment.

We are unable to determine from your letter what, if any,
violations of the FLSA are occurring at your place of employment.
I am enclosing a copy of the Handy Reference Guide to the Fair
Labor Standards Act. If after reviewing this publication, you
feel violations have occurred or you have any questions, you may
wish to contact our Albany District Office located at the Leo W.
O'Brien Federal Building, Room 822, Albany, New York, 12207.

Sincerely,

Arthur M. Kerschner, Jr.
Chief, Branch of Child Labor
   and Polygraph Standards

Enclosure

May 18, 1995
30 Lawn Street #2
Albany, N.Y. 12204

Inquiries
USDA
Agriculture Stabilization and
 Conservation Committee
Voohesville, NY 12186

Dear Madam/Sir,

The New York Times recently ran a report on the salvage of
food from a fire at the Americold facility in Kansas and let me
tell you, it was a real eye opener. The Times stated that this
was a storage place for food in the event of a national disaster.
My surprise comes from the fact that I've been living in this
country most of my life and I never knew we were squirreling food
stuffs away in mountain-side caverns in the mid-west.

I suppose it made sense back in the days of the Cold War,
when we didn't know if those crazy Ruskies were serious about
dropping a nuke on us or not. Hell, I kept a case of SPAM in the
garage for ten years in preparation for just that kind of
emergency. That stuff lasts forever, you know. It's toted as the
"other" processed meat product.

What I wonder is, do we need that kind of gastronomic
stockpile in the U.S. now? Also, do we here in New York State
have any "hidden refrigerators" tucked away in some obscure
place? If so, where? And what's in it? Are we saving up large
amounts of Swanson's frozen TV dinners in case of a huge
earthquake that wrecks all the fast-food joints? Are you saving
up any frozen pizza? If not, you really should. Even in the midst
of a huge disaster, Americans will be calling for their pizza. If
you want to be really safe, throw a few cases of Ben & Jerry's
Chunky Monkey Ice cream in there as well. Nothing like a nice
bowl of ice cream to soothe a nation during a big disaster.

I look forward to hearing from you.

Very truly yours,

J.W.Fagan

UNITED STATES
DEPARTMENT OF
AGRICULTURE

CONSOLIDATED
FARM SERVICE
AGENCY

ALBANY COUNTY CFSA OFFICE
BOX 497. 24 MARTIN RD.
VOORHEESVILLE. NY 12186

TEL: 518-765-3570
FAX: 518-765-2304

June 7. 1995

J. W. Fagan
30 Lawn Street #2
Albany. NY 12204

Dear Sir/Madam:

In regards to your recent letter concerning commodity warehouses in New
York State, the USDA Commodity Credit Corporation does employ private
warehousing firms to store processed agricultural commodities here in
New York.

These commodities would include such items as non-fat dry milk, cheese
and butter. These facilities serve several functions which include:

o   Storing food for school lunch programs, correctional facilities
     and the needed.

o   In the event of national emergency or natural disaster this food
     can quickly be dispensed to people in need.

o   Storage of Commodity Credit Corporation (CCC) purchases under
     USDA Price Support Programs. These purchases then become
     available for the above.

I have included a fact sheet on the United States Warehouse Act for your
information.

Thank you for your interest.

Sincerely,

FOR THE ALBANY CFSA COMMITTEE

Thomas Della Rocco
County Executive Director

TDR/jj
Enc.

March 29, 1995
18 B Old Hickory Dr. 2B
Albany, N.Y. 12204

Ann Fisher
75 Willett Street, Apt B1
Albany, NY 12203

Dear Mrs. Fisher,

I have to confess, I'm not a big believer in psychic powers.
A recent experience really stung and I'm hoping you can help.

My Aunt Tee is an intelligent woman, but came to believe
that a psychic could help her speak to her dead husband, Bucky.
Bucky Tee was a good guy, unfortunately had a habit of drinking a
lot and curling up any old place to sleep it off. One night he
chose a railroad track and it proved to be a bad choice. He now
sleeps with God.

Anyhow, this psychic (who will remain nameless, though until
recently ran a fly-by-night operation on Central Avenue and is
now out of business) told her that she could help. Adopting a
deep voice, she pretended to be "entered" by the dead Bucky and
really got Aunt Tee all kinds of upset.

Bending spoons, star maps and fortune cookies is all very
well, but this "communication with the dead" is quite
distasteful. How could anyone play with someone's soul like that
by pretending to be a dead relative or spouse to an emotionally
vulnerable person? Is there a professional accreditation a
consumer can look for to tell these bogus hucksters from the real
thing?

Very truly yours,

J.W.Fagan

Ms. Ann Fisher
75 Willett St. #1 B
Albany, NY 12210-1037

J.W. Fagan
18 B Old Hickory Dr. 2B
Albany,N.Y. 12204

Dear J.W. Fagan:

This is in reply to your letter of March29th.

I believe the woman you are referring to was Mrs. Anna.
She was a gypsy and they all do about the same thing. Usually
they say you have a curse and want a lot of money to remove
the spells put on you.

She was arrested and is not in the area now.

To tell the difference a gypsy will be for example:
Rev. Anna, Mrs. Anna, Sister Anna or Madam Anna. They all
go by first names and work on the outskirts of the city.
I believe cities do not let them into their limits.

A lot of this happened in the 1920'2 and 1930's but
a psychic who works with the police and has a good reputation
is one to go to.

Usually you can tell by their ads. They can change
negative conditions. They say anything can be changed on demand.

I am a medium so I know communication with the dead
is possible from a reliable person. Unless a person is a trance
medium you will not get the person's voice.

I get it through my mind. It is a bad g ame to hurt a
person so much. I agree with you fully.

This type of person does not last long in an area and they
have to make the money fast and run or be turned in to the law
and driven out.

There is not a professional accreditation yet. I went to
a ARE Conference at Va. Veach, Va. last year and they are working
on it.

I hope this helps you.

                        Sincerely,

April 4, 1995
18 B Old Hickory Dr. 2B
Albany, N.Y. 12204

Mary Rose Main
Girl Scouts of the U.S.A.
420 5th Avenue
New York, NY 10018-2702

Dear Ms. Main,

It has come to my attention that there may be a corporate fissure there at Girl Scouts, and it has manifested itself in the form of cookies. Bootleg cookies, that is.

My co-workers and I support Girl Scouts by purchasing many, many, many boxes of your scrumptious cookies. The favorite, by far, are the Somoas. Words fail to describe the bargaining power one holds in this office when waving a box of those tender confections.

In any case, one esteemed colleague came upon a package of cookies, apparently bearing the trademarks and authorization of the Girl Scouts, bearing the name "Caramel Delights" on an Orange box. The cookies tasted and looked like Samoa's (which as well as know come in a purple box) except they were laced with healthy doses of caramel. The taste was not offensive, and the evidence (unfortunately) was soon eaten. Lab analysis at this point, I'm afraid, is therefore impossible.

This has generated several discussions here regarding the existence of a Girl Scout splinter group, which seems to have broken off with the recipes and started producing their own cookies to cash in on the high demand. Has this happened? Are there rouge scouts out there, cranking out boxes of bootleg Samoas and pawning them off in front of grocery stores?

I felt inclined to bring this situation to your attention. If these splinter groups can successfully mass-produce the Samoas and package them attractively (with fifteen cookies instead of normal fourteen!) the old purple boxes of joy may be forgotten. Not only that, but what's to stop these rebellious campfire girls from selling the secret recipe to the highest bidder? And you know that Keebler Elf has been waiting for just this kind of opportunity!

I look forward to your reply.

Very truly yours,

J.W.Fagan

GIRL SCOUTS

April 26, 1995

J. W. Fagan
18 B Old Hickory Drive 2B
Albany, New York 12204

Dear J. W. Fagan,

Thank you for your letter to our National Executive Director regarding Girl Scout Cookies. I was asked to respond to your concerns as I oversee the Girl Scout Cookie Sale.

The Girl Scout cookies purchased by you and your coworkers were from girls representing two different local Girl Scout councils. Girl Scout cookies are baked by two different bakers, Little Brownie Bakers and ABC/Interbake Foods. Although the recipes are similar, Little Brownie Bakers produce Samoas and ABC produces Caramel Delights. Both bakers are required to produce three varieties of cookies that are similar. These cookies are staples of the Girl Scout Cookie Sale; Thin mints, Peanut Butter Sandwiches and Shortbread cookies. All the packaging is approved by the Girl Scouts of the U.S.A. and carries the Girl Scout trademark. Each council contracts with the cookie baker of their choice, so it is possible to have similar Girl Scout Cookies by different bakers in an area with two councils close by. There has been no division among the ranks or bootleg cookies being sold.

I hope that I have answered all your questions. Again, we would like to thank you and your coworkers for your continued support of Girl Scouting.

Very truly yours,

Kathleen P. Duncan

Kathleen P. Duncan
National Director
NATIONAL EQUIPMENT SERVICE
GIRL SCOUTS OF THE U.S.A.

KPD:cb

May 17, 1995
30 Lawn Street #2
Albany, N.Y. 12204

Kathleen P. Duncan
National Director
National Equipment Service
Girl Scouts of the U.S.A.
420 Fifth Avenue
New York, NY 10018-2702

Dear Ms. Duncan,

Thank you for your informative reply. My co-workers and I have taken your remarks under advisement.

I would like to remark, one business-savvy professional to another, that you are leaving a hole in your business big enough to drive a truck through. With so many bakers in on this deal, the recipes are bound to get seen by more people than I'm sure you would like. This weak link can be influenced by outside forces (the camp fire girls or the cub scouts clubs, for example) and your goldmine could be stolen out from under you.

Our suggestion would be for you to get all your bakers in a row and all your Girl Scouts in the fold. It sounds like you all need to be on the same sheet of music. This may all sound rediculous to you, but I could site you case after case of companies who were pillaged for having lax procedures and attitudes toward their golden egg-laying geese.

Very truly yours,

J.W.Fagan

January 15, 1995
18 B Old Hickory Dr. 2B
Albany, N.Y. 12204

Richard W. Carlson, President
Corporation for Public Broadcasting
901 East Street, NW
Washington, DC 20004-2307

Dear Mr. Carlson,

   To lay it right on the line, I don't like dealing with the employees, I like to deal with the boss. I have an idea that will finally get PBS the status it needs (deserves!) to compete in the modern channel-surfing world, and I wanted to send it right to the top.

   The news shows that I see on PBS these days are perhaps the best written, most impartial and in-depth programs on the dial. The only problem is, staying awake. The production is as sleepy as a Mid-West bus ride and it's really hard to get the meat of the story. The potential is there, though, which is far above the empty-headed news jockeys that spew forth on the other networks.

   So there's the problem. The solution? A Sixty Minutes-type format where McNeil and Leher grill politicians on their own turf! Surprise interviews in restaurants and bars, when the Honorable Gentleman from South Carolina has his guard down and a blond on his arm that his wife doesn't know about. Or, ambushes of camera and sound men in the parking lots, letting the public see their elected representative hide his face as he climbs into a gold-plated limo. Not only would this be a more appropriate forum to conduct conversations, but eliminate those prepared answers that your news shows seem to always get.

   I realize you face the challenge of standing watch on a ship that is not used to anything but the calm, placid waters of conservative journalism. However, I think you should at least investigate a more rough-and-ready format as a way to not only grab some of those channel surfer-dudes and dudettes, but to snag some juice exclusives.

   I'd be grateful to hear your thoughts on the issue, maybe you're one step ahead of me and already have a show like I described waiting in the wings?

                              Very truly Yours,

                              J.W.Fagan

CORPORATION FOR PUBLIC BROADCASTING

A Quarter Century of Quality Programming

Michael J. Schoenfeld
Senior Vice President,
Corporate Communications

January 25, 1995

Mr. J.W. Fagan
18 B Old Hickory Drive, #2B
Albany, NY 12204

Dear Mr. Fagan:

Thank you for taking the time to express your support for public broadcasting. I appreciate hearing from you.

As you know, CPB funding makes possible one of the most successful public-private partnerships in this country. Millions of Americans, like you, have invested a great deal in public broadcasting, and we intend to be the careful guardians of that trust.

CPB is committed to maintaining the integrity of public broadcasting. Certain things are important in this maintenance. Among these is the belief that public broadcasting should remain non-commercial. Another is the continued recognition of the local nature of public broadcasting.

As the debate continues, we are willing to listen to all suggestions that will work to improve the quality of public broadcasting. The American people have made an enormous investment over the decades. Your time and support demonstrates just that.

Sincerely,

Thanks for your idea — I have passed it along to the programming dept.

901 E Street NW
Washington, DC 20004-2037
(202) 879-9685

April 19, 1995
18 B Old Hickory Dr. 2B
Albany, N.Y. 12204

President
Association for Informal Logic
 and Critical Thinking
Baker University
Philosophy and Religion Dept.
Baldwin City, KS 66006

Dear Madam/Sir,

For years now friends and enemies alike have dreaded my
powers of persuasion. Using carefully crafted arguments and
verbal traps I lure in the unsuspecting victim into a corner and
WHAM! I lower the boom.

Because of this, I received much reproach about my demeanor.
My argument remains that as long as I can prove my point and back
it up in some way, the validity holds true. My critics call my
comments slanderous and unconchonable, causing distress and ill-
feelings for no good reason. Please take under advisement that
these observations of my persuasive short-comings originate from
the mouths of belligerent fools.

What can I do to explain to these fools that logic is not a
popularity contest, that you have to "call them as you see them"?
How do I show them the merits of alternative and sometimes loose
interpretations? Are there any techniques to this? Please keep in
mind we are dealing with simpletons.

You prompt attention to my dilemma will be most appreciated.

Very truly yours,

J.W.Fagan

AILACT

The Association for Informal Logic and Critical Thinking

April 27, 1995

J.W. Fagan
18B Old Hickory Dr. 2B
Albany, NY 12204

Dear J.W.:

In the literature of argumentation, the model of Socrates is prominent. He is seen as a great teacher because of his humble manner and his ability to listen to a person, ask appropriate questions, and help people understand the limitations of their espoused position--hence furthering inquiry.

I would suggest that you and your friends buy copies of the Platonic dialogues and form a summer reading group, carefully going through them. Another alternative might be to buy copies of a critical thinking text and work as a group through the text. That way you all would understand the rules of a critical discussion.

I am enclosing a page from a text I have written.

Sincerely,

Donald L. Hatcher
AILACT Treasurer

March 22, 1995
18B Old Hickory Dr. 2B
Albany, NY 12204

Mr. Brian Dyson
Coca-Cola Enterprises, Inc.
1 Coca-Cola Plaza, NW
Atlanta, GA 30313

Dear Mr. Dyson,

"Coke is the real thing!" was the anthem of your company during most of my childhood, and the commercials - although folksy and bland - were unoffensive. Now I see Coke is spewing out all kinds of wacky commercials, and it's not that entertaining.

First, there's a polar bear theme which I really don't get at all. Bears can't purchase cola products, nor can the hold a bottle opener or figure out the concept of twist-off caps. Then there are those mini-stories of "me and my kid sister" about how a kid wants a brother and gets a sister instead, and how she wrecks his life but now that they are grown up they drink Coke and hang out. What's up with that?

In this age of "channel surfing" and "holistic therapy" the consumer doesn't need to be confused or befuddled. They want to be entertained, amused and above all they want to laugh out loud. Bust a gut! Life is crappy enough without having to put up with a cutsey polar bears drinking Coke.

I hate to mention the P-word, but have you seen the latest Pepsi commercial? They unveiled two at the Superbowl and both were hilarious. One has a guy trying to feed a dollar into a soda machine, the other is about two truck drivers for Coke and Pepsi becoming friends, only to tear up a diner over a can of Pepsi. Now I hate Pepsi, but I had to laugh at those.

As I said, I love Coke and you don't have to worry about losing me as a loyal customer over a few cheesy ads. But, I thought I might chime in about the sorrowful state of your recent ads in hopes of prodding some yucks out of your future productions.

Very truly yours,

J.W. Fagan

The Coca-Cola Company

COCA-COLA PLAZA
ATLANTA, GEORGIA

ADDRESS REPLY TO
P. O. DRAWER 1734
ATLANTA, GA 30301
1-800-438-2653

March 29, 1995

Mr. J.W. Fagan
18B Old Hickory Dr., No. 2B
Albany, NY 12204

Dear Mr. Fagan:

Thank you for your letter addressed to Brian Dyson regarding our recent advertising and the advertising of our competitors. We appreciate your sharing your comments with us.

Mr. Fagan, as you probably know, our advertising is very important to us. Therefore, we are grateful when our consumers take the time to share their thoughts with us. Please be assured that your feedback has been shared with the appropriate management.

We hope your next favorite commercial will be one of ours. In appreciation for your comments, please enjoy the enclosed coupons. Best wishes to you!

Sincerely,

Melissa Packman

Melissa Packman
Senior Consumer Affairs Specialist

MP:mp

Enclosure: Coupons (2)

MANUFACTURER'S COUPON | NO EXPIRATION DATE

Compliments of The Coca-Cola Company

FREE:
Your choice of one of the products
listed below in one 6-pack of bottles or cans:

Coca-Cola classic®
caffeine free Coca-Cola® classic
diet Coke®
caffeine free diet Coke®

cherry Coke®
diet cherry Coke®
TAB®
Sprite®

diet Sprite®
Mello Yello®
diet Mello Yello®
Fresca®

Minute Maid® soft drinks
diet Minute Maid® soft drinks
Fanta®
Mr. PiBB®

BRAND AND PACKAGING AVAILABILITY VARY BY MARKET.
SEE BACK OF COUPON FOR REDEMPTION INFORMATION.

May 19, 1995
30 lawn Ave. #2
Albany, NY 12204

The Boring Institute
PO Box 40
Maplewood, NJ 07040

Dear Madam/Sir,

The significance of this missive is to ascertain the mission
of your provocatively titled "Boring Institute". The reasons to
sustain such an institute escapes and defies my reasoning.
Hopefully, you will be able to clear the air.

Boring is as boring does, a wise man once said. That is,
ironically enough, quite a boring thing to say since the whole
concept of such an institute is droll, bland, tiresome and
tedious. To construct a whole existence of membership around such
a philosophy is, not to beat a dead horse, boring. Worse than
boring, which is a step below watching a solitaire tournament on
t.v. with the sound off.

My question is this: what possessed you? Isn't the world
crippled enough with droll soap operas, B-movies and talk shows
that deaden the brain worse than lead paint fumes? Why embark on
such a counter-productive, imbecilic and ineffectual pursuit when
there are other "fish to fry"?

Very truly yours,

J.W. Fagan

May 19, 1995
30 lawn Ave. #2
Albany, NY 12204

The Boring Institute
PO Box 40
Maplewood, NJ 07040

Dear Madam/Sir,

The significance of this missive is to ascertain the mission of your provocatively titled "Boring Institute". The reasons to sustain such an institute escapes and defies my reasoning. Hopefully, you will be able to clear the air.

Boring is as boring does, a wise man once said. That is, ironically enough, quite a boring thing to say since the whole concept of such an institute is droll, bland, tiresome and tedious. To construct a whole existence of membership around such a philosophy is, not to beat a dead horse, boring. Worse than boring, which is a step below watching a solitaire tournament on t.v. with the sound off.

My question is this: what possessed you? Isn't the world crippled enough with droll soap operas, B-movies and talk shows that deaden the brain worse than lead paint fumes? Why embark on such a counter-productive, imbecilic and ineffectual pursuit when there are other "fish to fry"?

Very truly yours,

J.W. Fagan

Lucky for you, I rescued your letter before a small, furry animal ate it!

A.C.

BORING!!

THE BORING INSTITUTE

ALAN CARUBA
Founder

Box 40
Maplewood, NJ 07040

201/763-6392

Dear Friend:

Thank you for your interest in **The Boring Institute.**

Founded in 1984, the Institute has become one of the nation's most popular media spoofs. We start each year in March spoofing the Academy Awards with our own **Most Boring Film Awards,** followed in September by our spoof of the new TV season with our **Fearless Forecasts of TV's Fall Flops.** The Institute receives international media coverage each year for our list of **The Most Boring Celebrities of the Year** each December.

Each July, the Institute sponsors **National Anti-Boredom Month** to focus media and public attention on the serious side of boredom; its many links between personal and social problems that include school drop-outs, marital problems, job stress, crime, and additions that include food, alcohol and drugs. Boredom pre-states depression and is a factor in suicide.

The Institute publishes a widely recommended guide, **Ten Secrets to Avoid Boredom,** ($3.50) which opens into a poster with nearly 70 ideas of things to do. For fun, there's our official, two color **Boring Certificate of Associate Membership** ($5.00), the perfect gift for the favorite boring person in your life.

Best wishes!

Sincerely,

Alan Caruba
Founder

ALAN CARUBA   Box 40   201/763-6392
Founder   Maplewood, NJ 07040

Want to "join" The Boring Institute?

You can! For only $5 you can have your very own "official" Boring Certificate of Associate Membership.

Or you can be the proud recipient of an "official" Boring Award. Also only $5.

And here's the best part...since the Institute doesn't publish a boring newsletter or hold boring meetings... you will probably never hear from us again!

Send your check or money order to:

The Boring Institute
PO Box 40
Maplewood, NJ 07040

8½ X 11
Two color

June 26, 1995
30 Lawn Street #2
Albany, N.Y. 12204

Steve Wagner
Society for Eradication
of Television
P.O. Box 10491
Oakland, CA 94610-0491

Dear Steve,

For years I have been an advocate of tossing all of the TV's in the creek and getting this civilization back on track. Up until now, I thought I was alone.

I grew up without television. My little brother put a hammer through "Tony the Pony" one Saturday morning and in the process killed the tv. I was a young child of 11 years, and my Dad was sick of finding us glued to the tube like mesmerized robots, and so never got it fixed.

As a result, I became a great reader. I read cereal boxes, paperbacks, newspapers, slasher novels and even some racy romance stuff. I was exposed to a vivid "theater of the mind", bare of idiotic energizer bunny ads, Suzi-chap stic commercials and cookery infomercials.

Something ought to be done. The minds of our young are being sucked out like yolk from an Easter Egg. The "MTV" generation, as they are called, resent the old and care only for themselves. They have been nursed, baby-sat and taught by a money-driven, mind-bending and sexually explicit device spawned by suit-wearing satans. Our future is doomed. I'm glad I'll be dead before Madonna buys her way into the White House.

Very truly yours,

J.W.Fagan

August 14, 1995   OK
30 Lawn Street #2
Albany, N.Y. 12204

Steve Wagner
Society for Eradication
of Television
P.O. Box 10491
Oakland, CA 94610-0491

Dear Steve,

What's up there? I directed a missive towards you two months
ago and haven't heard back from you. I'm very discontented.

It would seem to me that your group would be gladdened to
have supporters as dedicated me on your side. I happen to be a
very important person here in "the house" and could really put
your group on the map, so to speak. Or, at least assist you in
spreading the "anti-tv" directive.

I can understand you being quite busy with this mission, but
at least you can show the common courtesy of a return letter.

Very truly yours,

J.W. Fagan

RECYCLOGRAM:

J.W.: SORRY -- WE THOUGHT WE'D
ALREADY SENT SOME INFO. LATEST
NEWSLETTER IS ENCLOSED. WE'LL
RE-SEND PREVIOUS IN A COUPLE
OF DAYS.
    YES, WE'RE GLADDENED TO
HAVE SUPPORTERS SUCH AS YOU.
"BUSY", HOWEVER, IS NOT THE WORD
FOR IT. "INUNDATED" MAY BE A
LITTLE CLOSER TO THE MARK.
    BEST WISHES,
    STEVE (4 S.E.T.)

June 1, 1995
30 Lawn Street #2
Albany, N.Y. 12204

Mr. Fred Turner
McDonald's Corporation
One McDonald Plaza
Oak Brook, Il 60521

Dear Mr. Turner,

Over the years, I've enjoyed many a Big Mac attack. Growing up, it was a real part of our lives.

We used to stop by the local Mickie-D's before going out on Friday nights, have in-depth discussions and an occasional rumble in the parking lot. In Cloverdale, near where I grew up, it was the place to be seen and heard. There, and the feed and tack shop.

Time went by and McDonald's served many purposes. It became the oasis from dorm food at college, a friendly meal in strange foreign countries, or just a place to get a real Shamrock Shake around St.Patty's Day.

Now, I can't go there anymore. The salt on your french fries has driven me away. Not just the one down the street, but I have noticed increased sodium chloride layers on the fries over the past year all over the area. I'm not a health freak trying to watch my salt, mind you. These things are so crusted that they are un-edible. When I pull a fry out of the box and hold it up to the light it sparkles like a diamond. I'm sorry, I just can't eat them like that! .

I've tried asking for no salt, but that seems like too much for the assembly line-minded workers. Finally, with many regrets, I've resigned to going to the home of the whopper, where they let <u>you</u> add salt on your fries, if you so choose.

From sharing my peeve with friends, others have echoed my concerns. Even my softball team, which used to celebrate with a round of Quarter-Pounders with Cheese meals, now eats at the place that serves square burgers. Disappointing, but they also do not pre-glaze their fries with salt.

I hope from this missive your company decides to rid the golden fries of the crusty confection which is keeping those of us who prefer the golden arches from going there.

Very truly yours,

J.W.Fagan

McDonald's

McDONALD'S CORPORATION
OAK BROOK, ILLINOIS 60521
708/575-6198

June 28, 1995

Mr. or Ms. J.W. Fagan
30 Lawn Street #2
Albany, NY 12204

Dear Mr. or Ms. Fagan:

Thank you for taking the time to contact Fred Turner. He asked me to respond to your letter on his behalf. I appreciate this opportunity to address your concerns about the added salt on our french fries.

Be assured, we're very sensitive to the dietary needs of our customers. We closely monitor trends and changes in America's eating habits, and make changes and enhancements to our menu. As you're aware, salt can be omitted from our french fries upon request. However, I apologize for any inconvenience you've experienced when requesting this service in the past.

We value your feedback, and have shared your comments with our Product Development team for their review.

Once again, thank you for sharing your thoughts with us. I hope you'll use the enclosed gift certificates the next time you visit McDonald's. We would welcome another chance to serve you again soon.

Sincerely,

McDONALD'S CORPORATION

Liz Williams
Office of the Senior Chairman

enclosure: $3 gift certificates

February 14, 1995
18 B Old Hickory Dr. 2B
Albany, N.Y. 12204

Consumer Responses
The Quaker Oats Co.
PO Box 049003
Chicago, IL 60604

Dear Madam/Sir,

Those little snack bars of yours really pack a punch.

While skiing in the Canadian Rockies, my party became
stranded on a ski lift after it stopped half-way between the mid-
station and the peak. The area was under a white-out alert, and
we couldn't see anything except that we were in deep s**t. We
huddled together on the quad chair trying to keep warm and
praying that the lift would start up again before we became human
popsicles.

Well, the sun soon went down and we realized we were on our
own. Hunger set in and my brother Pat started making cannibal
jokes. Then I reminded him that the younger the meat, the better
it tastes, and he shut up. We checked out pockets and a lone
Quaker Oats Chewy Granola bar was produced. It was to be our last
supper.

It became light out again soon after that, and the lift
began moving again. When we reached the top we learned that we
had only been stuck for a half hour. An eclipse had occurred in
the meantime, throwing off our sense of time. We were just happy
to be alive. Although we'll never know, I for one think that
Chewy Granola bar would have kept us from succumbing to the
frost. For a few hours, at least.

Very truly yours,

J.W.Fagan

Consumer Affairs Center
The Quaker Oats Company, P.O. Box 049003, Chicago, Illinois 60604-9003

February 28, 1995

J.W Fagan
2B
18 B. Old Hickory Dr.
Albany, NY 12204

Dear Consumer:

Thank you for contacting us about Quaker Rice Cakes.

Our objective is to produce high-quality products that our consumers enjoy. There are many ways of measuring success but none are as gratifying as hearing directly from you. Your opinion helps us to know that our products meet our consumers' needs and preferences.

The comments of our consumers are always welcome and we appreciate having them on record.

Amy Gibson
Consumer Response Representative
Consumer Response Group

AG/bao

January 4, 1995
18B Old Hickory Dr. 2B
Albany, NY 12204

United Airlines
Customer Relations
PO Box 66100
Chicago, Il 60666

Dear Madam/Sir,

The older I get, the less I seem to enjoy to eat. On a
recent flight on one of your planes, however, I had a meal which
absolutely stunned my taste buds. I loved it.

With the limited culinary capabilities of an airplane
considered, my meal was better that most stuff I get in real
restaurants. The presentation of the meal was pleasant, a chunk
of roasted chicken floating comfortably on a bed of white rice,
complete with green beans, a sauce of some sort and a shortbread
cookie. I washed it all down with a perfectly chilled mini-bottle
of Chardonnay Blanc which was a surprising delight all to itself.

I thought it was going to be too small to fill my usual
ravenous apatite, but the meal settled in nicely and a couple of
nice after dinner shots of Jameson whiskey ended a wonderful
repast and sped me into a peaceful slumber which endured until we
gently bumped upon the runway at out destination.

My question to you folks is this; are these meals available
to the common joe? Can I order some of these succulent offerings
so I can bring them into work and enjoy here on the ground? Or
will I have to "fly the friendly skies" to taste a meal like that
again?

                              Very truly yours,

                              J.W. Fagan

UNITED AIRLINES

January 19, 1995

Mr. J.W. Fagan
18B Old Hickory Drive 2B
Albany, NY 12204

Dear Mr. Fagan:

Thank you for your letter of January 4. We're pleased to
hear you enjoyed our meal service during your recent travel
with us.

Most of our meals are supplied through our caterer Dobbs
International. I'm sure if you write directly to them and
give them your flight information they would be able to
assist you. You may contact them at: Dobbs
International//5100 Poplar Avenue//Memphis, TN 38137.

Your business is important to us and we look forward to
serving you in the future.

Sincerely,

Mary Bucher
Customer Relations

REF #: 1043807A

MAB/cl

February 12, 1995
18B Old Hickory Dr. 2B
Albany, NY 12204

Mary Bucher
Customer Relations
UNITED AIRLINES
PO Box 66100
Chicago, IL 60666

Dear Ms. Bucher,

Greetings and best wishes in this new year!

It was great to hear from you and receive the information on Dobbs International, whom I have written in hopes of procuring culinary information. I hate to intrude on your kindness, but I have another question which you may be in a position to answer.

Due to a childhood incident involving a Canadian Goose and some rope, my sister Anney is reluctant to try flying. Admittedly, the modern airplane is hardly an unsafe mode of travel. One only has to read any article in the newspaper on a crash where they always point out that you have a better chance of being hit by a garbage truck being driven by a Jewish Rabbi on a city street than to be killed in an airline crash.

Unfortunately, those childhood scars run deep and Anney is wary even of elevators. I'd love to come up with a way of showing my sister that it is not only MUCH faster to travel cross country than the bus, but more comfortable, too. And, I think you get to meet an overall better quality of people in the air. Certainly they are better groomed, etc.

Could you suggest a really safe, easy flight that I could break her in with? I travel the Rocky Mountain route a lot and I think that will be a bit bumpy for her first trip. My hope is that I can help not only to bring her into the 1990's with a modern mode of transport, but also to help heal that minor incident of poor judgment on my part way back when.

I'd appreciate any suggestions, but maybe a route with a nice movie would be best. You know, to help take her mind off the height thing. I look forward to hearing from you.

Very truly yours,

J.W. Fagan

UU UNITED AIRLINES

February 22, 1995

Mr. J.W. Fagan
18B Old Hickory Drive 2B
Albany, NY 12204

Dear Mr. Fagan:

Thank you for writing - it is so nice to hear from you
again. I have enclosed a brochure which I think may be of
some help to Anney. I recommend a nice flight from New
York to Chicago. Chicago is a fun city - it's a relatively
short flight and you don't run into too many headwinds.

Good luck to you and your sister and have a great and
healthy New Year!

Sincerely,

Mary Bucher
Customer Relations

REF #: 1056980A

MAB/cl

August 13, 1995
30 Lawn Street #2
Albany, N.Y. 12204

Customer Service
American Touristor
91 Main Street
Warren, RI 02885

Dear C.S.

As a world traveler I have encountered many strange lands,
harrowing scrapes with unlearned peoples and more common thieves
than you could shake a walking stick at. Through it all, my
American Touristor luggage has carried my possessions safely,
securely and comfortably.

In the former East Germany, the border guards tugged at the
finely-stitched seam of my bag, looking for contraband (they
didn't find it) while in Canada, the brutish customs agents
played a twisted game of soccer with my case. He and a pal
laughed cruelly as they punted my poor bag between them like a
miss-shaped soccer ball. The case did not give them the pleasure
of breaking open and displaying my underwear to the world.

Perhaps the biggest test was the unruly Bermuda officials
that subjected my case to the "Drop Test". While anchored in
Hamilton, they selected certain cabins on the boat and raided
them, taking bags and heaving them over the promenade deck rail
onto the pier below where supposed drug-sniffing dogs peed on
them. After a brief rinse in the shower, it was good as new.

I plan to take my bags on a sojourn of the Amazon next year.
Perhaps you could suggest a few new models that would fill my
luggage needs for this journey. Something not only durable, but
fireproof, I suppose. Any ideas?

Very truly yours,

J.W.Fagan

J.W. —

Per your request, please find the latest offerings from A.T. They are not fireproof, but will protect you from most snakes if you close yourself up inside of it.

Good luck,

Vic Lud

March 20, 1995
18B Old Hickory Dr. 2B
Albany, NY 12204

Mr. Peter Berlin
Shoplifters Anonymous
380 N. Broadway, #206
Jericho, NY 11753

Dear Mr. Berlin,

My friend (ex friend) is a vicious stealer. He rips off just about anything that isn't bolted to the floor, and some things that were. I was told you may be able to offer a few hints in dealing with this crazed lunatic.

I haven't a clue what got him started in this life of crime, but for the longest time everything was fine. Then he started coming home with groceries under his clothes. "I'm conserving paper by not using a shopping bag." he says. "Baloney!" I said.

That wasn't all. One day I saw his bedroom door open and inside were mounds of clothes with the tags still on. They weren't even his size! He also gets companies to send him those collector plates through the mail and then keeps them without paying. Yesterday he got a religous plate depicting Rosa Mystica levitating over water.

I want to help him and salvage this relationship. He always pays his rent on time and people like that are a hard find. What do you suggest?

Very truly yours,

J.W. Fagan

SA | SHOPLIFTERS ALTERNATIVE®

The Educational Alternative

March 29, 1995

Mr. J. Fagan
18B Old Hickory Drive, 2B
Albany, NY 1204

Dear Mr. Fagan:

We are pleased that you decided to contact the SA Help-Line because you have taken an important step toward making a positive change in your friend's life.

We will do everything we can to assist him/her to overcome their shoplifting problem. However, you must know up front that we can only help your friend if he/she is truly ready to accept help. In other words, he/she must be ready to help themselves.

The first step is for your friend to take the educational Home Study segment of the SA Course, which he/she does at home using two cassette tapes, a workbook and an answer sheet. The course helps people to understand their problem, teaches them how to weigh the risk vs. reward and describes what actions they can take to stop their impulsive behavior...so that they never get involved in shoplifting again. The SA Course should take him/her about 5 to 6 hours to complete.

Your friend keeps the two cassette tapes and workbook and returns only the answer sheet to SA for evaluation. We'll then send him/her a letter with our recommendations and, if he/she wishes, a copy to his/her attorney or the court.

Because shoplifting is more severe for some people than for others, the home study course may not be sufficient. If your friend feels he/she wants more help after taking the SA Course, he/she can call us on our toll-free line and we'll then discuss what his her next step should be. There is no charge for this service.

Please be aware that all mail coming from this office will not be identified as coming from Shoplifters Alternative but rather from the SA Educational Series. So, as long as your friend is the only one who opens their mail, no one will know what's inside.

He/she may register for the SA Course by completing the enclosed Registration Form and returning it to us with a tuition fee of $48.00 payable by check, money order or Visa/Mastercard in the enclosed prepaid envelope. Just follow the simple instructions on the Registration Form.

Please note that the SA Course is designed and used primarily for shoplifters who have been caught and instructed by the court to take the SA Course. Therefore, you will find some reference to the court throughout the literature.

If you have any questions, please call us toll-free anytime at 1-800-848-9595.

We look forward to receiving the Registration Form and helping you make a positive change in your friend's life.

Sincerely,

SHOPLIFTERS ALTERNATIVE

March 11, 1995
18 B Old Hickory Dr. 2B
Albany, N.Y. 12204

Matlock
100 Universal City Plaza
#507-3E
Universal City, CA 91608

Dear Mr. Matlock,

As a fan for many, many years now, I pride myself in following these amazing stories of your life. The other residents here also enjoy it, but I have to explain it to them.

I wanted to tell you that the tall lady a few weeks ago was lying to you when she told you that man she was kissing was her cousin. He was not! As soon as you left the room they went off together. I couldn't see the ending of the story because of a disruptive person, so you may have found that out by now. I hope so.

Can I ask if you still work as a lawyer or just act out your stories now? I may have a case for you. That disruptive person I mentioned may have done-in someone here who hasn't shown up for a week. I'm still trying to get evidence. Let me know if you'd care to come here and check around.

Very truly yours,

J.W.Fagan

(NO REPLY RECEIVED)

April 14, 1995
18 B Old Hickory Dr. 2B
Albany, N.Y. 12204

al-Thani, Sheik Khalifa bin Hamad
The Royal Palace
Doha, Qatar

Dear Al,

Our class recently had career day, and I was so inspired by
a tv show about your land that when asked what I wanted to be
when I grew up, I answered, "I want to be an Emir!".

That didn't go over too well at first, but I persisted and
my teacher assigned me the task of gathering all the info I can
on how you become an Emir, and what an Emir really does. Who
better to ask, I thought, than you?

In books I've read that you run the country like our
President does, except you still wear swords. That's cool. I
think everybody should settle their problems with swordplay as
opposed to guns, don't you? I also think those pajama-like
clothing you wear is more comfortable for everyday work. When I
grow up, I don't want to wear a tie. Already I have to put them
on for Christmas and Easter and they suck.

What can you tell me about what you do? Does the job include
public appearances and stuff like it does for politicians here?
Do you get elected or do you have to have revolt to get into
power? If so, how do you start one?

Let me know as soon as possible. My paper on this is due in
June.

Very truly yours,

J.W.Fagan

(NO REPLY RECEIVED)

Dear Mr. Fagan,

With your permission I'll send you the Foley-Belsaw Career
Kit on how you can become a professional locksmith. This
is your opportunity to make good money doing light, digni-
fied work, in the Albany area.

> According to the Locksmith Ledger, a nationally
> known trade journal of the industry, the average
> wage for a locksmith is now $25.00 an hour!

Good money yes, but certainly not the whole story. You
can also make 50% to 100%, or more mark-up on parts and
supplies you sell, as a routine part of your service.

You can complete your training in six months or less at
home without giving up your present employment. The
course is not expensive. As a matter of fact, most of
our students earn while they learn. Many earn enough to
pay for the entire course and more.
But, right now, all you have to do is:

> 1) Tear off the form at the top of this letter.
> 2) Enclose in the postage-paid envelope.

We will send your Foley-Belsaw Institute Career Kit by
First Class Mail. No salesman will call on you. There
is absolutely no obligation to buy anything.

Sincerely,

George Doetzl, Director
FOLEY-BELSAW INSTITUTE

P.S.: Please return form at top of this letter before
date shown on front. That way you will have your Career
Kit in plenty of time to make your decision on whether
to enroll in the upcoming class.

PROFITS from locksmithing service and repair can provide...

...CASH for future security or supplemental income
...CASH for travel, vacations, fishing trips
...CASH for the things you've always wanted

January 11, 1995
18 B Old Hickory Dr. 2B
Albany, NY 12204

George Doetzl, Director
Foley-Belsaw Institute
6301 Equitable Road
Box 419593
Kansas City, MO 64141-6593

    Dear Mr. Doetzl,

    I received your generous offer for an exciting career
as a professional locksmith. With the kind of luck I've been
having, I was hoping something like this would come along!

    Not to bore you with petty details of my turbulent
life, but times haven't been rosy here in New York. A
staggeringly unfortunate series of mishaps involving a irate
college administrator, a backhoe and a rather embarrassing
anxiety attack have left me with a tattered college career
and a pair of worn trousers. As well, my love life is in the
crapper because my girl ran off with an aluminum gutter
salesman.

    The pictures included in your note indicates that a
locksmith gets to work with lots of folks (two of the three
scenes featured hot-looking women!) and I would really like
that. Also, you stress that you deal with CASH, which is
definitely the way to go these days. Lord knows I've written
a rubber check or two in my days.

    It sounds to me like this could really turn my train
around and head it in the right direction. Please send me
all the free stuff you have, as well as any personal advice,
hints or handy tips. I'm really in debt to your fine
company. I eagerly await your reply!

                            Very truly yours,

                            J.W. Fagan

(NO REPLY RECEIVED)

June 22, 1995
30 Lawn Street #2
Albany, N.Y. 12204

William J. Hyble
U.S. Olympic Committee
1750 E. Boulder Street
Colorado Springs, CO 80909

Dear Mr. Hyble,

Congratulations on choosing Utah as our next host state! You all must be very happy and proud to have beaten out some tough competition for the honor. Good job.

As a footnote, I would like to suggest my humble city of Albany for future consideration as a Olympic City. I realize the U.S. may have to wait a few years before we can snag another chance as a host city, so I'll submit Albany now.

There's a saying here that goes, "We've got it ALbany" (get it? ALL-bany). It also won some kind of honor as an "All-American City" a few years ago, though now I'm not sure from what. It was a big deal at the time, maybe you heard about it?

What we have is a river on our doorstep which would be perfect for swimming events. As long as the races are in June or later, since winter debris (trees, dead fish, ect.) sometimes hangs around until then. The PCB problem has largely fixed itself, and by the year 2010, you may be able to eat what you catch.

For winter events you have to go no further than State Street. In previous years, the City's fathers trucked in snow from outlying areas and turned the street into a giant ski slope. The hill starts on the steps of the Capitol Building and careens wildly down to Broadway Ave, several blocks below. This would make for a great slalom and/ or bobsled course.

There's much, much more. Washington park is capable of holding Equestrian and distance races, while Crossgates Mall would make an excellent host for track and field events - climate controlled, of course.

I will put myself at your disposal for questions, comments and all the free tickets to the future Olympic games that you can send my way.

Very truly yours,

J.W.Fagan

(NO REPLY RECEIVED)

J.W. Fagan
Box 134 Rt.41
Greenville, NY 12083

William Wrigley, CEO
Wrigley Gum Company
410 N. Michigan Ave
Chicago, IL 60611

Dear Mr. Wrigley,

May I say it is a distinct pleasure to be directing a missive your way, sir. I have been eating your gum since I was a small boy.

Eating? That's right. Although I have heard all the wives' tales, like "If you swallow your gum it'll sit in your stomach for 10 years!" and "You'll choke in the night, you'll see!" I have persisted in eating chewing gum through my turbulent adolescent years and right into adulthood. As far as I can tell, it hasn't hurt me. Or so I thought.

After a particularly bouncy hockey game some time ago, I noticed a slight lump on my rib cage. Being a tough guy, I shrugged it off. But a month later it was still there, and slightly bigger. It didn't hurt, it was just there. I went to my doctor and her ran a battery of exams with more poking and probing than I care to describe here. The end result was one baffled physician. He's seen tumors, and this is no tumor. It's not a bruise, growth, melanoma or a boil. His x-rays show a grapefruit sized ball of something just inside the lower ribcage near the colon.

My imagination immediately began conjuring up visions of a soft-ball sized wad of gum sitting in there! Reluctant to bring this theory before a medical professional I would like to know if you, in your long years in the business, have ever encountered such a thing. If so, are there acids or laxatives to relieve such a condition? I really would hate to have to go under the blade for something like this.

I eagerly await your reply.

Very truly yours,

JW Fagan
January 29, 1996

Wm. **WRIGLEY** Jr. Company

WRIGLEY BUILDING • 410 N. MICHIGAN AVENUE
CHICAGO, ILLINOIS 60611

Telephone: 644-2121
Area Code 312

WHOLESOME • DELICIOUS • SATISFYING
February 13, 1996

Mr. J. W. Fagan
Box 134, Route 41
Greenville, NY   12083

Dear Mr. Fagan:

Thank you for writing to Mr. Wrigley to ask about the
digestibility of chewing gum. Our company president has been out
of the office on business, so rather than further delay a
response, I'm happy to reply to your concerns.

Many people seem to harbor misconceptions about chewing gum, and
we've received many letters over the years asking about the
digestibility of our product. To give you some background,
chewing gum is made of five basic ingredients -- sugar, corn
syrup, softeners, flavors and gum base (the insoluble part that
puts the "chew" in chewing gum). The first four ingredients are
soluble and are extracted from the gum as you chew. Gum base,
however, is not. And while the majority of our consumers
recognize that our product is not intended to be swallowed, if
gum base is swallowed, it passes through one's system as other
roughage does, such as popcorn. This normally takes only a few
days.

Although we can't draw any conclusions about your condition, if,
upon further examination, your physician detects a relationship
between what you have described in your letter and our product,
please let us know. We will pass along that information to our
medical director for his evaluation.

Incidentally, chewing gum is a food product, so all ingredients
used in it may be used in chewing gum in compliance with U.S.
Food and Drug Administration regulations.

We hope this information is helpful. Please let us know if we
can be of additional assistance. Thanks again for writing.

Sincerely yours,

WM. WRIGLEY JR. COMPANY

Barbara C. Zibell
Consumer Affairs Administrator

BCZ/sl

J.W. Fagan
Box 134 Rt.41
Greenville, NY 12083

President
Cider Mill Company, Inc.
898 Main Street
Acton, MA 01720

Dear Madam/Sir,

Yesterday, I purchased your Dog Trolley (100') and brought it home to my family. I set up the Trolley as per the instructions on the back of the package. They were very clear, and it took no longer that a half hour to set up. My dog, Smoot, watched patiently. Although a puppy, she is 40 pound of mischievous pup and so she was curious as to what I was doing probably to see if she could find a tool to steal to hinder my progress.

After giving the cabling a few hard tugs to check it's integrity, I hooked up Smoot and she ran around getting used to her new device. She would run full speed the length of the cable, then veer off and reach the end of her lead. It would snap tight, jerking on her lead and causing her to literally flip in the air head over heels and onto her back. She paused and repeated her actions, as if to enjoy it. After an hour of this curious behavior I went inside and got my wife to see what she thought about it all and she got very nervous after just one demonstration by Smoot, so we took her off the Dog Trolley and took her back into the house where she promptly knocked over a lamp.

This morning I hooked her up to the line and watched her run playfully up and down. Then, she sprinted for the other end and clothes-lined herself again! It was actually too painful to watch her repeat that again, so I had to remover from the device entirely.

I'm at the end of my rope with this, so to speak. Do you have several customers reporting this same problem? What advice do you give them?

Very truly yours,

JW Fagan
March 24, 1996

J.W. Fagan
Box 134 Rt.41
Greenville, NY 12083

President
Cider Mill Company, Inc.
898 Main Street
Acton, MA 01720

Dear Madam/Sir,

Yesterday, I purchased your Dog Trolley (100') and brought it home to my family. I set
up the Trolley as per the instructions on the back of the package. They were very clear,
and it took no longer that a half hour to set up. My dog, Smoot, watched patiently.
Although a puppy, she is 40 pound of mischievous pup and so she was curious as to what
I was doing probably to see if she could find a tool to steal to hinder my progress.

After giving the cabling a few hard tugs to check it's integrity, I hooked up Smoot and
she ran around getting used to her new device. She would run full speed the length of the
cable, then veer off and reach the end of her lead. It would snap tight, jerking on her lead
and causing her to literally flip in the air head over heels and onto her back. She paused
and repeated her actions, as if to enjoy it. After an hour of this curious behavior I went
inside and got my wife to see what she thought about it all and she got very nervous after
just one demonstration by Smoot, so we took her off the Dog Trolley and took her back
into the house where she promptly knocked over a lamp.

This morning I hooked her up to the line and watched her run playfully up and down.
Then, she sprinted for the other end and clothes-lined herself again! It was actually too
painful to watch her repeat that again, so I had to remover from the device entirely.

I'm at the end of my rope with this, so to speak. Do you have several customers reporting
this same problem? What advice do you give them?

Very truly yours,

JW Fagan
March 24, 1996

Dear JW —
We have not had problems with this in
the past. I suggest you work with your dog to train her. If
this does not work you should purchase a tieout with a
spring to ease the snaping when she is stopped by the
tieout. This will help a little. Please call if we can
help you further. Thank you.

Jeff Chizmas
1 (800) 523-6995.

RECEIVED MAR 27 1996

J.W. Fagan
Box 134 Rt.41
Greenville, NY 12083

Customer Service
Hormel Foods Corp.
Corporate Office
Austin, MIN 55912

Dear Madam/Sir,

I have just used your "Real Bacon Bits", and I hope I don't regret it.

This evening my wife and I entertained a visiting foreign dignitary and his entourage providing a seven-course meal which included a large salad featuring your bacon bits. While cleaning up, my wife noticed there was a small packet in the now-empty jar of pork bits which had the words "Fresh Pax" on it. In smaller type was the warning, "DO NOT EAT - CONTAINS IRON". Panic stricken, I checked the remains of the salad and found no other Fresh Pax. Scarcely a leaf of our tossed delight was left in the bowl.

The image of our guests pitching forward in convulsions while in transit to their home was distressing enough for us to call them on their car phone and warn them that there may have been some Fresh Pax in their salad, and that they needed to see a physician immediately. All six detoured to the nearest emergency room and had what was left of a delightful Roast Duckling meal pumped unceremoniously from their stomachs.

I don't need to tell you that they will never "break bread" in this house again, and we feel that your Bacon Bits share no small portion of the blame for this. Why couldn't your packaging be more forthcoming about the dangers within? And why the hell are the Fresh Pax in there in the first place? And why not call them some more accurate, like "Dangerous Chemical Poison Pax" instead?

These are questions I feel your company should provide comment on.

Very truly yours,

JW Fagan
March 17, 1996

Consumer Affairs

Hormel Foods Corporation
1 Hormel Place
Austin MN 55912-3680

March 26, 1996

 J Fagan
P O Box 134 Rt 41
Greenville, NY 12083

Dear   Fagan,

Thank you for contacting us about HORMEL Bits.

A small packet of minerals has been placed in the package
to help keep it fresh. This packet assures the product
will maintain the quality which you expect from Hormel
Foods. The mineral packet contains a form of iron oxide
which is not harmful. However, it is not meant to be
eaten. The packet should be thrown out after using the
product.

We regret your unfortunate experience. However, our
production plants are inspected by the USDA and we are in
compliance with all USDA regulations. The USDA only allows
safe substances to come in contact with food products.

Please feel free to contact us again if we can help you
further.

Sincerely,

Connie Gilsrud
Consumer Response Specialist
960401150

$1.00   MANUFACTUR
$1.00   MANUFACTUR
$1.00   MANUFACTUR
          EXPIRES Dec
$2.00   MANUFACTUR
          EXPIRES Dec

Hor
Fo

Consume

$2.00   © Hormel Foods

J.W. Fagan
Box 154 Rt.41
Greenville, NY 12083

Customer Service
Connectix Corp.
2655 Campus Drive
San Mateo, CA 94403-9817

Dear Madam/Sir,

In the interest of goodwill, may I extend the findings of my experience with your product
"Ram Doubler". You see, I would like to give you some free advice, in the interest of the
common good of the Joe-Blow computer people out there. My idea? I think you should
remove "Ram Doubler" from the shelves and rename it "Demonic Possession". Why? Let
me tell you.

I loaded your product onto my machine not looking for a miracle, but maybe a little better
performance from my windows system. My equipment and OS setup fell easily within
the "recommended" configurations on the box. However, when I rebooted after loading it,
I received more than what was described in the manual.

"RAM DOUBLED!" Exclaimed a gray box in the corner of the screen. Cool. Let's try
Microsoft Word. Oh-oh. General Protection Fault briefly flickered on the screen and then
over my computer speakers came the words "RAM DOUBLED!" in a booming, deep
male voice which made me jump up and kick the dog. Then the screen was back at the
program manager.

Weird. I un-installed and re-installed the product. After rebooting, I tried America On-
Line and when I tried to sign in, I heard the ominous "RAM DOUBLED!" mantra again
and the screen flashed a quick message about a failure in the device on comm port 2. And
then we were back at the old Program Manager. I clicked on the setup.exe in file manager
to un-install this Beast and I heard an echoing, cackling "HA HA HA HAAAAAAA!"
sound bite which made my skin crawl. I checked all my WAV files and neither that laugh
or the ram doubled files were anywhere to be found.

I un-installed from a DOS prompt and every thing works like it used to. Are these "Bells
and Whistles" some kind of joke you have in your do-nothing program? If so, you guys
are sick. Keep the forty bucks. Seek therapy.

Very Truly Yours,

JW Fagan

February 2, 1996

J.W. Fagan
Box 134 Rt. 41
Greenville, NY 12083

Dear J. W.,

I am sorry to hear that your experience with RAM Doubler for Windows was not a positive one. I am curious as to what version of Ram Doubler you are running. The latest version of RAM Doubler for Windows is version 1.03.

RAM Doubler for Windows version 1.03 has been released. It is posted on AOL, Compuserve, and the Web. To get the RAM Doubler 1.03 updater from Compuserve:

· Use the "Go" command:Connectix
· Enter Library 3
· Download and decompress the file "RDW103.EXE" and Readme.

From America On Line you can download it from the Connectix Forum. Open "Software Libraries", "updates and Patches" and download the updater. It has numerous fixes and may help.

From the Web:
http://www.connectix.com and it is the RAM Doubler for Windows v1.03 updater.

If you do not have access to AOL, Compuserve or the Web, then email with your home address and I will send you the update.

We have been unable to reproduce the effects you cited in your letter. In consultation with our engineers, I verified that we have included no wave files or sound drivers in our program. We will continue to research these problems. Any additional information that you can supply us will be greatly appreciated.

The GPF you report occurs with which version of MS Word? What is the wording of the GPF you received? How much RAM do you have? What kind of machine is it? I know this is a lot of information, but it is needed to properly diagnose your problem. Any extra information will be greatly appreciated. Also, please attach your original problem with the information. We would like to know where you purchased your version of RAM Doubler for Windows. Please email me if you can, for that is a quicker way to respond. Otherwise, you can call me at 1-800-9500-5880 or 415-571-5100.

On behalf of the entire team here at Connectix, thanks for all your feedback.

Respectfully,

Bill Callow Jr.
Windows Tech Support
(callow@connectix.com)

Connectix

2655 Campus Drive

San Mateo

California

94403

tel: 415.571.5100

800.950.5880

fax: 415.571.5195

J.W. Fagan
Box 134 Rt.41
Greenville, NY 12083

Bill Callow Jr.
Connectix Corp.
2655 Campus Drive
San Mateo, CA 94403

Dear Bill,

I try to ask simple question and you tear into me like a starving dog into a tube steak. Just hold on a second, Buddy!

For one thing I don't doubt your "engineers" have had a hard time reproducing this effect. What I did have a hard time believing was that your engineers put down the hacky-sac long enough to even look at their product. IT DOESN'T WORK. I tried it on TWO different PC's in TWO vastly different environments. One machine was a domestic, mid-range model with 8 meg, and the other a high end model with 24meg. There is only one thing common about the two machines.... the only change in performance was the words "RAM DOUBLED" on the corner of the screen!

You may be Mr. Know-It-All out there in the Shaky State, but your tone doesn't work with me. The smoke-screen you try to create by bringing up the version of MS-Word I'm using, or my current hardware configuration is irrelevant! The product crapped out, and you're looking anywhere but at the source of the problem. I deal with end-users every day in support of a e-mail system which spans thousands of users and 15 states. What does that mean? Absolutely nothing! I just felt like adding it in here.

Your wishes on behalf of the Connectix team are falling on non-RAM Doubled ears. But, thanks anyways.

Very Truly Yours,

JW Fagan

PS - I hope your desk is near a nice, solid doorway. The "Big One" is just around the corner.

Feb 29, 1996

J.W. Fagan
Box 134 Rt. 41
GreenVille, NY 12083

Dear Mr. Fagan,

I appreciate your feedback regarding our RAM Doubler for Windows 3.1 product.
I am disappointed that you have not been able to experience the satisfaction that
other RAM Doubler customers have had with the product. I have spoken with
hundreds of our customers that have seen the true benefits that RAM Doubler
brings to Windows 3.1.

I want you to know that we are still committed to working with you to resolve the
problems you are experiencing on your system. I have been very impressed with
our technical support staff and their ability to solve customer issues. If you have
not spoken with them on the phone please call them toll free at 1-800-950-5880.

However, if you truly feel that our product has no value then please return it for a
full refund. I have taken the time to obtain an RMA return number for you.
(RMA# - RM3997) If you send back the original diskette, manual, and receipt
with this RMA number written on the outside of the package we will send you a
full refund.

Connectix stands behind all of its products with a satisfaction guarantee. If you
are not satisfied we will happily refund your money.

Sincerely,

Bryan Mayo
Product Manager, Windows Utilities
Connectix Corporation

J.W. Fagan
Box 134 Rt.41
Greenville, NY 12083

Floyd Dykeman
WJIV Radio
3 Computer Drive West
Suite 126
Albany, NY 12205

Dear Floyd,

We were touched by the warm welcome conveyed by your direct-mail advertisement that came to us by way of our mailbox. Nice of you to say hello.

Being new to the area, we have found that living here in the country is certainly different than the smelly city we just came from. Gone are the idiotic honking taxis at all hours of the night, the drunk college kids jumping into the neighbors pool with their clothes on, the tinkle of broken glass of an expensive foreign automobile which is almost certainly followed by the screaming of rubber as the thieves spin their stolen wheels. And, of course, who can forget the annoying newlywed couple upstairs who are up until all hours of the night "consummating".

The first few nights here my wife and I barely slept. It was if we had fallen into a void of time and space where no sound existed. We had to get up and put on my videotape of "Best Daytona 500 Moments" with the sound at medium just to get some winks. Slowly we weaned ourselves, the volume on the TV getting set lower and lower until now we don't even need that.

Now it seems we are challenged by a different sensory accostement. In the past two months, Three different pairs of Jehovah Witnesses (isn't it a little suspicious that they need to be in pairs? I always feel peer pressure) had knocked on the door and forced their way into the house. After demanding a cup of tea, they proceeded to lecture us on our evil ways, and how we ought to come down to a "meeting" and meet their "friends". I've done some reading in my day, and I know all about cults! They aren't going to get ME to one of their "meetings". My wife neither!

You mentioned in your letter that you have a group going there "The WJIV Prayer Warriors". Maybe you and your gang could stop by and we could clear the air with those witness fellows, huh? Sure could use the help.

Very truly yours,

JW Fagan
March 11, 1996

WJIV–101.9 FM RADIO

SERVING THE GREAT NORTHEAST

(518) 437-1251   Office
(518) 437-1252   Fax

April 3, 1996

J W Fagan
Box 134, Rt. 41
Greenville, NY   12083

Dear Brother:

    I appreciate your letter and by the time you receive this letter,
I have no doubts that you will be well adjusted and getting your
normal rest.

    The Jehovah Witnesses are all over witnessing, they have a quota
to meet and you are one of theirs to try to get to. I am please that
you are well aware of cults. In this day and age there are many deceivers
in all shapes and sizes. I appreciate your invitation about the "Prayer
Warriors". We aired your letter on "Share Time" as we do, and now the
"Prayer Warriors" are praying for your situation, so expect a change.

    Brother Fagan, thank you again for writting, it is very much
appreciated. I hope your move will be a blessing to you and your
wife.

                    In His Service,
                    WJIV Radio

                    Floyd Dykeman
                    Floyd Dykeman, President

FD/am

3 Computer Dr. West Suite # 126 Albany, New York 12205

Order Form

✦✦✦

Brighten someone's day! Send them their very own copy of

LETTERS OF A MALCONTENT

Please send postal order to:

SMILING DOLPHIN PUBLICATIONS
BOX 581
GREENVILLE, NEW YORK 12083

Please direct orders via the Internet to:

DOLPHINPUB@AOL.COM

PAYMENT:
CHECK OR MONEY ORDER
MAIL ORDER PRICE <u>$9.95</u> (New York State residents
please include 8% sales tax.)

SHIPPING:
BOOK RATE $1.75 FOR FIRST BOOK AND 50 CENTS FOR
EACH ADDITIONAL BOOK. SURFACE SHIPPING MAY
TAKE THREE TO FOUR WEEKS FOR DELIVERY. AIRMAIL
IS $3.00 PER BOOK

Please Send Me _____ copy(ies) of Letters of a
Malcontent. I understand I can return the book(s) for a
full refund - for any reason, no questions asked within
60 days of purchase.

Please indicate if you wish a signed copy.

Name_____
Address_____
City_____ State_____ Zip_____